PREFACE

"I lay no claim either to literal ability, or to botanical knowledge, or even to the best practical methods of cultivation," a woman of great gardening wisdom once began an essay, and that was fine for her to say because it was humility, pure and simple. But if I tell you that in my case these same claims do indeed hold true, you can trust it. While a painting of modest Gertrude Jekyll's well-worn gardening boots hangs in the upper-crusty Tate Gallery in London, my sorry L.L. Bean specials will never make their way to anywhere but the local dump.

But what I do share with Jekyll—the person regarded as most responsible for the renaissance of classic garden design in the twentieth century, whose writings I could read and read again—and I trust with you, too, is a wonder at the very existence of plants.

How can it be that they have such intricate beauty: have you ever seen the clever paintings that live inside a flower? How is it that so many garden plants can disappear come winter and then, from nowhere, reappear in spring, unbeaten by having "lived" like Birds Eye vegetables in the earth's own freezer, month after frozen month?

How can it be that a border of daffodils blooms each spring in the woods above my rural home, although the people whose house they once adorned are decades gone? And why does a tomato smell great, and its foliage just smell, and why aren't every plant's leaves—the centers of photosynthesis—the color green? It is this natural curiosity, coupled with the need to touch and smell and otherwise get to know these living things, that counts foremost, all manner of scientific degrees notwithstanding.

This instinct of botanical wonder, at least in my case, came from many sources, all close to home— from the zinnias my Grandma Marion cut and stuffed into the Fiestaware bowls of water, flowers that picked up the brightest flecks in the old linoleum of that kitchen, painted, walls and ceiling and cabinets, in yellow high-gloss. Beneath the old, contorted wisteria, there was an iron padded chaise at Grandma's, too. They plopped me on it for my birthday photo, while all around me wisteria pods fell onto the canvas upholstery and onto the slate floor beneath. Manna from heaven. Happy birthday, Margaret. Welcome to the garden.

Digging down deeper into the psychological subsoil will take some time—read on. All I can tell you now are fragments like that one; flashes of memory, moments of recognition. All I can say for certain is that it is gardening that I love more than anything, and here is a simple example of the reason why.

Just the other night I reached into the freezer for a plastic container of "tomato junk," a hodgepodge I use as the stock of my winter diet. It is a commingling of whatever edible was still standing and producing when frost closed the last season down— this year the junk contains tomatoes, beans, parsley, kale, and squash. There, like a reddish brick of ice in my hand, and then a few hours later in its next incarnation as the base of lentil soup, my garden was with me again.

Gertrude Jekyll, in uncharacteristic immodesty, called herself a "garden-artist," but do not look in this place for any such lofty figure. Simply, I like two things very much: the smell of freshly washed laundry and the smell of warming earth that is hit by a rain shower. Hence down deep I am part washerwoman, part ditchdigger, and thankfully it is a true symbiosis. The former helps undo the filthiness the latter wreaks on the hands.

No, neither my garden boots nor my garden is the stuff that art is made of, a fact for which I am only partly apologetic. My garden is where I can be myself—perhaps the only place besides the pay-by-the-hour couch that invites me to be so, in fact. This is where I think big, where I overdo it, where I don't turn inward and downward but really stretch myself—never mind the insecurities.

In the untidy maze of garden this wintry weekend, the zinnias will be waiting, dried and shrunken to a dilapidated state of brown, as contorted by months of cold days and nights as Grandma's wisteria was by age. I did not cut my zinnias to fill the bowls as my ancestor did, at least not in the season's final month. In my kitchen, the bowls hold shallots and garlic, a 'Blue Hubbard' and a buttercup squash, all destined for the winter kettle. My zinnias, doornail dead, and nearby the coneflowers and rudbeckias and all, have a higher final purpose.

To the birds, each dried seed head is a minifeeder, and as the sun comes up upon these frigid mornings I am content to sit and watch the goldfinches having at it, bursting from one botanical snack bar to another with zeal such as I feel only when . . . to tell the truth, I never get quite that energetic anymore.

My bird feeding, next to my gardening, is what amuses my friends most, though frankly I see nothing funny in it. When other gardeners' checking balances are finally spared the growing season's near-daily drains for pots and plants and seeds, there I am in my woolens, hurtling up to the Agway farm store, possessed by a mantra of "seed sale . . . seed sale . . . seed sale." When others are clipping supermarket coupons to stretch the household budget, I am urging the birds around my place to "eat, eat, eat," in hopes of moving one hole closer on the Birdseed Club punchcard to that as-yet-elusive, free 20-pound bag.

"We are building a habitat," an old friend used to needle, impersonating my voice and using my very words, as we'd dig yet another hole for a berry-bearing shrub or drive yet another feeder pole into the good earth. But underneath the kidding he knew that it is the magical intertwining of things that gets to me—we feed the birds in the lean times; they eat our bad bugs and thus there's a harvest.

And the bottom line is that is what I am doing when I am gardening: building a habitat. It is a place for me, and for my friends, and for our friends the birds and bugs, and, yes, even the blubbery woodchuck who rambles down the hillside from time to time in fairer months, in search of a refill for his sagging belly.

Lately, it has been the place for a hungry stray farm cat, too, a truly wild creature, and when I throw a little stone close by to chase him from beneath my sacred feeders, I feel a twinge of sorrow, for after all he is just trying to join in the cycle, too.

Margaret Roach
Copake Falls, New York

INTRODUCTION A garden without a gardener is a jungle waiting to happen. A gardener without a plot to till is likewise a very sorry sight. This book is about both sides of the equation: the delicious organism that gardener and garden, once united, quickly become, as they ride the peaks and abysses of what the weather and life dish out. That said, this is also a

basic garden book, but then again it is not so basic. It will supply guidance to those looking for the way to transplant a tomato or prune a hydrangea, but it also shares some of the guidance from the other side of the equation: the advice and insight that I, as a gardener, have gotten in return from my plants.

Because I think of my garden and myself as the two main components of the same organism, I also think about the gardening year in a way that may, at first, seem a bit unfamiliar, or even odd. You will not find chapters on spring, summer, fall, and winter here, or any named for the calendar months, either. To my mind, those expected divisions of the year are better used to track sales figures for a line of dresses (if you happen to be a fashion house, that is), or stashing away bits of paper for the inevitable day when your taxes must be prepared.

Keeping mental and emotional track of what is going on outdoors is not so dull, or unromantic. Instead, I imagine that the garden's year is roughly parallel to the six seasons of life, from conception through birth and on to youth, adulthood, senescence, and death/afterlife. For people, moving from phase to phase takes years (if all goes well) and there is only one guaranteed chance at each; in the garden, the life cycle is packed into a single year, and then the next, over and over, even long after the gardener is gone.

In my system, each of the six phases is roughly equivalent to two calendar months. For example,

Conception is equivalent to January and February, a time when we are conceiving of the garden to come by planning on paper and ordering seeds (two of the many topics covered in that chapter). By the time we get to Death and Afterlife, it is November and December. We gather up the debris and make compost (the only eternity I feel certain of), pile on some mulch, and carefully store away any seeds we saved during garden cleanup (another way that next year's garden rises up out of the one gone by).

I find this anthropomorphic view of the garden comforting, to be honest, a handle to hold on to when trying to remember what to do when and what's coming up in the list of garden chores. It also reminds me that gardening is not just a hobby, like building model airplanes or stamp-collecting. The medium is alive and always changing and, no, you are never really in charge for a second, no matter how straight your rows or how sturdy your stakes. Something larger is always at work, something no mere gardener can control.

This volume also differs from your garden-variety garden book, and that is in the highlighted plants. If you're going to go to the considerable trouble of digging a hole, I figure, why not fill it with something extraordinary? With this in mind, I have skipped over some of the mainstays (read: stereotypes) of the garden world in favor of things I like a whole lot better, and have enjoyed tracking down and growing. You will see many of them in the photographs here by my companion, Kit Latham, all but a couple of them taken in the garden around the home we share as it passes through the cycles itself, as he and I watch and even make some contributions every now and again.

HOW I CAME TO GARDEN

I came to the garden in my twenties, at a time when things were not going so well in the people parts of life.

My new friends the plants helped me through a long spell facing an impossible responsibility: how to ethically, sensitively care for a relative who would never get well, but would live a very long time. Each quart pot of some unknown creature (at this stage, even common names were Greek to me, and Latin was unthinkable) was a reason to rouse myself for another day. The young plants needed me, after all, and I them. They were promise, and possibility.

Now, when I conjure in my mind's eye the garden that I made in those five or so years, I have to laugh. Set around the home I grew up in and had returned to after a decade's absence, the garden was (as my father labeled agreeably eccentric people) a real pip. At the feet of the aged privet hedge, 6 feet high and more gaps than foliage, I tried determinedly to coax a carpet of annual lobelia (*Lobelia erinus*), the sprawling kind with blue flowers normally used in hanging baskets and window boxes. There was virtually no soil left around the dense root system of the old privet, but I was insistent that the blue flowers would make a swathe the length of the hedge row, and used the strongest, sharpest trowel in the garage to gouge out tiny pockets to stuff the transplants into. A chisel and crowbar might have made planting easier.

I was incredulous when the lobelia refused to grow. The little plastic labels imprinted with the pretty picture of all those flowers said that light shade was suitable, and that's what I had given them. It didn't mention that 1 cubic inch of loose soil wasn't enough for any plant, or that root competition from a 50-year-old hedge probably wasn't lobelia's cup of manure tea, either.

The hedge continued in its role as "test kitchen" when I took saw and loppers to it a year later in my first attempt at "Rejuvenation of an Aging Shrub"— another important garden lesson, and the next subject in my impromptu home-study course in horticulture. My self-styled curriculum in "Annuals as Ground Covers" hadn't gone so well—the lobelia didn't even make it a month, let alone fill in and bloom—but I was undeterred. Gardening was my personal occupational therapy, my sedative, and I persevered.

My very first experiment might have been called "Introduction to Sculptural Plants." For a steep hillside bed by the driveway, I'd chosen a palette of hens-and-chicks (*Sempervivum*) and red-hot pokers (*Kniphofia* species), and who knows why. But how I loved this peculiar, even pitiful pairing—the lurid orange-and-yellow pokers jutting upward from the sempervivums. Perhaps I thought the hens-and-chicks needed a rooster, and there is something vaguely birdlike about the red-hot pokers, which are also terribly masculine. How ugly my combination was. How proud it made me to see it grow.

Or take my first significant encounter with perennials, evidence of which is still inscribed in pencil inside the back cover of the first gardening book I owned, *The Victory Garden* by James Underwood Crockett. Once I calculated how much it would cost at $3.99 or $5.99 a pot (vintage prices!) to actually plant even a modest border, I apparently decided to grow my own from seed. Between the closeups of flowers in his book and those in the delightfully gaudy Thompson and Morgan seed catalog, I had drafted a list of a dozen perennials to grow. "Leave no color unturned" must have been my motto then, judging by the list (you may wish to put on your sunglasses to dare conjuring it, even in your mind's eye):

Maroon and gold *Gaillardia*, lavender Canterbury bells (*Campanula*), white balloon flowers (*Platycodon*), reddish pink *Dianthus*, a fuchsia-colored bee balm (*Monarda*), hot red Maltese-cross (*Lychnis chalcedonica*), red and yellow columbines (*Aquilegia*), pink foxgloves (*Digitalis purpurea*), multicolored *Lupinus*, pale blue perennial flax (*Linum*), purple pansies (not even a perennial, but what did I know?), and fire-engine-red painted daisies (*Pyrethrum*).

Ugh.

Nevertheless, I ordered them all and began collecting yogurt cups, milk cartons, and other cast-offs as potential seedling pots. (To this day, not a single garden of mine has included those plants, proof that the trauma, although suppressed, remains imprinted in my psyche.)

There was, of course, no spot in the house suitable to support thousands of plantlets that wouldn't be ready for the open ground for more than half a year. And I didn't even know enough to consider selecting a combination of plants that might achieve a succession of bloom over a long season, or anything else that goes into making a garden.

I did it all wrong: wrong plants, wrong propagation setup, and I even started every seed in every packet—as if I could use 100 or 80 or 300 of something. In those days, results didn't really matter. I was hooked on the hopefulness that working with plants gave me. I loved those spindly seedlings fiercely, as they taught me my early lessons on the life (and, unfortunately, death) cycle of plants.

Today, new faces in the catalogs and at the nurseries still tug at me to take them home and love them. But it is more an addiction to the larger process of the garden year's cycle, so much like my own life's course, more than any one plant, that keeps me at it.

We have begun to grow up together, the garden and I. It is now about 20 years since I tortured that first flat of blue lobelia. These days, in a garden I have been at nearly a decade, I try to be kinder, in respect for what the world outside my windows and doors has given me. What follows, then, are some of the lessons learned so far—plants, processes, tips, and tricks—to help you through the seasons of your garden, and your life.

Conception

We have found neutral ground, my sister and I. After three and a half decades, there is at last a place for us to be at peace, a new mother tongue that does not have so many angry phrases. We talk not of what has been, or might have been had someone or the other done something differently. We speak the language of flowers instead.

"I have an urgent garden question" is how her phone calls begin these days, and with those words we start rewriting the story of big sister–little sister, a tale that did not go so well the first time around.

No matter that she doesn't always listen—she stored the dormant pot of calla lilies under the kitchen radiator, not exactly where I had recommended, but they bloomed just swell the next year anyhow. Her "urgent" questions are the opening lines of our revised first chapter of growing up together, so I am not so picky about such details.

When we were little, and the grandma she is named for grew them, my little sister crinkled her freckled nose and objected loudly to the stink of marigolds. Their gaudy color shone—positively gleamed—as if Grandma had planted them exactly to match the child's orange hair. Young Marion was more inclined to horseplay than to horticulture, however, her knees skinned and trousers shredded not from bending to the task of weeding but from some far more hellish undertaking decidedly lacking in adult supervision. No time to stop and smell the flowers when you are playing cowboys.

Though not her namesake—perhaps they should have called me Lily, as hard as I tried to be demure—I never declined a chance to sit by Grandma Marion while she dried flowers in an old wooden press. From the lifeless bits, she composed intricate arrangements—"pressed-flower pictures," we called them, proudly, and I remember that it was my room, not Marion's, whose walls were covered in them.

Later, when Grandma was gone and growing pains were being felt full force at my end of the hallway, Marion was the sister who got bouquets from those who wished for her attention. Even then, Marion loved a rose—preferably long-stemmed and by the dozen—but I never actually thought that she would *grow* one. I had something to learn about my sister, and about humility.

"Are those roses you gave me *ramblers*?" she asked not long ago, because they had clambered up and over this and that as rambling roses do. "You know, the ones you said were *dead*?"

The plants in question had arrived in time for an unseasonably early bout of high heat. Because I was not home, they had sat in their package in the sun, right where the UPS man left them. Attempting a rescue on my return, I soaked them awhile in a bucket of water and cut the cooked parts back, but they were, to my impatient eye, too far gone.

"I'll take them," said Marion, seeing the "dead" creatures lying on the lawn one day when she visited, and so she did. Within what seemed like no time, the dead plants had undergone a resurrection, and then proceeded quickly to ascend, too. By

summer's end, they were well up a trellis, where an enthusiastic tangle of vines—probably previous years' casualties from my own garden—grew.

There is a certain hazard to passing on your outcasts. You may very likely have to face the plants again; do not forget this fact. Some, sent away because they were so aggressive, will quickly overtake their new home, too, which does little to enhance the sense that the spirit of generosity was behind your gift.

Others may warrant banishment because their color proves too jarring; no spot for them can be found. Such was the case with a dozen peach- and melon-colored daylilies, and I was glad to see them go. I was not quite so glad to see them as a focal point at Marion's, where somehow, magically, they fit right in as if custom-ordered for the spot.

It is not all having to grit teeth, of course, not all a test of one's semi-good humor. I admit to an intense pleasure when she comes to pick my apples in fall, knowing I will hear about the pies and sauce for months to come.

For now, the phone keeps ringing with the questions, although I suspect she doesn't really need the answers anymore, and could even give a few herself. Admittedly, I will not try storing my callas inside the radiator cover, but there is a certain red poppy in her garden I'd like.

We are actually beginning to look more alike as a consequence of this shared passion. In our case it is the matching scratches on the insides of our forearms I refer to, the marks of rose thorns, or the ankle-encircling scars from wasp nests run over with the mower. Even our gardens have taken on a certain similarity: she, too, is inclined to pumpkins in her flower beds.

There is more to this gardening stuff than planting, I guess, more than step-by-step detail. No wonder, then, that the language of gardening and the language of life have so many words in common: words like *tend* and *cultivate,* words like *grow.*

Though not her namesake—perhaps they should have called me Lily, as hard as I tried to be demure—I never declined a chance to

CATALOGS The cheapest gardening education can be had in the pages of plant and seed catalogs. At the start of one's gardening life, a good catalog will be one that's full of color photos, such as that offered by Thompson & Morgan for seeds or White Flower Farm for plants and bulbs, the same way that baby's first books are a bit on the gaudy, raucous side. By year two or three,

though, if all is going well, it's time to screw up the courage to shop from the nonillustrated listings—J. L. Hudson, Seedsman (seeds), for example, or Heronswood Nursery (plants). (See Sources.)

First, nonillustrated catalogs make you really read the entry and see if a plant is right for your conditions, rather than get all excited by a color close-up of a flower that won't work. Second, the people behind the more hard-core catalogs are typically connoisseurs, so you'll be selecting from among the newest and most appealing plants available. These experts will usually share their growing experiences, cultural tips, and successful plant combinations. Third, and most important, these are the kinds of lists that require you to sharpen your Latin skills, which anyone intending to make gardening a habit must accomplish. Common names aren't useful; they are imprecise and may vary according to local tradition. And often more than one plant has the same common name. Did you want false indigo the perennial (*Baptisia australis*) or false indigo the small tree (*Amorpha fruticosa*)? The two are hardly interchangeable, any more than I am the same person as another Margaret just because she happens to have the same first name.

When I started gardening, just two catalogs came in the mail, but as soon as I placed an order the number began to soar. Many were worthless, but I knew I was making progress when I was able to discern which were which—when I could identify the real gardeners behind the best of the lot from the mass marketers behind the rest.

Today I happily subscribe to more than 1,000 catalogs, for everything from pumpkin seeds to palm trees to garden furniture and greenhouse supplies. I use most of them in the course of my garden-writing work, not at home, where I don't even have a greenhouse. As winter reading, though, they are unsurpassed, and I always discover something new to get excited about.

A home gardener needs far fewer; three to four dozen will do, if they are the right ones. Consider them your ongoing correspondence course in horticulture. Send for them now to start getting ready for the coming season.

PLANNING ON PAPER
The people who helped me learn to garden—whether in books and catalogs or at lectures and classes—always said the same thing: put it all down on paper before you plant, even before you purchase a single seed packet or a single pot of anything.

I quickly came to wonder if I would ever really be any good as a gardener, because try as I might, I simply could not force myself to map out planting plans ahead of time. Shop the nurseries, yes. Order by mail, definitely. But figure out in advance what I planned to do with it all? Never.

To me, planning on paper in winter is about as satisfying as eating a February-issue tomato—mealy and insipid at best. In January or February, I am as impatient for the payoff—the real thing—as a child whining from the backseat on a long car trip: "*Are we*

sit by Grandma Marion while she dried flowers in an old wooden press. From the lifeless bits, she composed intricate arrangements—"pressed-flower pictures," we called them, proudly . . .

there yet?" No amount of paper and crayons (or even a grown-up notebook and pen) will quiet me.

I firmly believe my own adage "You have to grow it to know it," by which I mean there's no substitute for the education a gardener gets from actually bringing a plant home and trying it. Through such experimentation, develop a repertory of plants that work for you, and you will be able to make a garden in time. That's basically how my theory goes; the more plants I learn about, the better chance I have of knowing one for each situation I confront in the landscape.

There are, however, a few instances when even plantaholics such as myself need to plan beforehand on paper. The vegetable garden requires such advance calculations, every single year. Conceiving a vegetable-garden plot is best done in the downtime just after New Year's, when the arriving catalogs start the gardener's botanical clock ticking.

First, make a list of what you want to grow and, more important, how much of each plant you want to grow. Just because seedlings tend to come in cellpacks of four or six of a variety doesn't mean you need that many. And the number of potential plants in a seed packet is almost always way too high.

No one needs to grow even six *cherry* tomato plants, but if you like homemade tomato sauce, or plan to can tomatoes, you'll want at least six *paste*

tomatoes—perhaps more. A half-dozen basil plants at harvest time yield enough pesto for a large family for the entire year; if you plan to use the herb mainly as a garnish, grow one plant. For frying, roasting, and stuffing, four or six pepper plants might not be too many. But how many jalapeños can a person eat? Figure on one plant, if you like them at all; I set out two, which more than fills two large canning jars with pickled peppers to use in Mexican-style dishes throughout the year.

To map out my vegetable garden, I work on graph paper. Make a roughly-to-scale plan of your vegetable beds once on the graph paper, then photocopy it and keep the master for subsequent years. Using a scale of one foot to one box on the paper is easiest, or tape together two or four pieces of paper and change the scale. Work in pencil, since things will change a dozen times before they are right (and another time or two when you actually get outdoors in spring). The hardest part is allowing proper spacing, so think of it simply: each plant gets a square-shaped space of its own, which may be equal to a quarter box (a 6-inch by 6-inch plant, such as lettuce, arugula, or broccoli raab), one box (a 12 by 12 plant, such as a heading lettuce), a box and a half square (peppers, eggplants, broccoli, cabbage), or two boxes by two boxes (zucchini, for instance, or tomatoes, which I grow in cages, although staked tomatoes would need only a box and a half square). With the smallest plants (carrots, for instance, or beets, which require only a couple or a few inches square), allow a row half a box wide and figure two parallel, staggered rows will fit into that amount of space.

Compute the space a plant needs by reading the seed packet for that particular variety, since not all varieties of the same crop have the same growth habit. Seed catalogs are a real help here: the entry on each crop in catalogs like Johnny's Selected Seeds or

LEFT **Cherry tomatoes, not yet ripe.** RIGHT **The pond garden and upper meadow under a blanket of snow.**

Parsley (shown here, the flat-leaf Italian kind) makes a handsome, edible edge for vegetable-garden beds.

Southern Exposure Seed Exchange address issues such as spacing. Figure in enough blank space to allow you to move through the garden, even when the plants are at their lustiest and encroaching on the paths. Beds can be as wide as 4 to 5 feet if you can reach them from both sides; against a fence or anywhere else where there is no path or access point on one side, they should go no wider than 3 feet.

Maximize the growing space by using salad greens or herbs such as parsley and bush basil as an edging, for instance in front of a row of tomatoes, instead of giving them a separate bed of their own. Use bush beans the same way. And plan to make subsequent sowings anytime a bit of space becomes available—a technique called succession planting (see page 109).

Besides the vegetable garden, large areas of ground cover and other mass plantings also require some thinking ahead, especially when you will be ordering a large number of one or several unusual varieties that can't easily be supplemented on the spot—or returned. Find out the mature width of each plant, which it usually takes about three years to reach. If you can wait, use that figure as your spacing between plants; if you want faster coverage, you may plant closer (as much as twice as close, for nearly instant coverage). For example, plants that will grow to 18 inches across in time would normally be spaced 18 inches apart to allow for their mature size; for quicker coverage, you might plant them a bit closer in each direction (say, every 12 inches, or even every 9 inches). Once you've settled on a particular spacing, multiply that number by itself to calculate the number of square inches each plant will require.

Now you're ready for higher math. Determine the square footage of the area you wish to cover, which is easy with rectangles and squares (multiply length times width) but not so obvious with circles (multiply the radius times itself, and then multiply that total times 3.1416, or *pi*), or ovals (figure out the average radius, and proceed as for a circle). If the area is amoebic, try to see it as a puzzle made up of pieces shaped like squares, rectangles, and circles or ovals, and compute the size of each piece, then add them together. Once you have your total square footage, multiply it by 144, which is the number of square inches in a square foot, to get the number of square inches of plants you need, since plant sizes and spacing recommendations are usually expressed in inches. Then divide the number of square inches per plant into the total of square inches in the bed to determine how many plants you'll need. Add 10 percent to your order to make up for ones that will need replacing. It may sound daunting, but in the era of calculators, it requires only patient inputting to come up with the right answer.

Designing a really good, large-scale mixed border (a blend of perennials, shrubs, bulbs, annuals, and biennials), the way the English seem to be able to do as a birthright, would justify the use of paper and pencil, too. This is particularly important if you are trying to accomplish a succession of bloom over a long season and with a range of heights and colors, the grail of such plantings. In that instance, use several or more photocopies of the same to-scale garden outline, each one to represent what would bloom in, for example, early spring, late spring, early summer, and so forth, representing the "layers" or stages of the planting.

On my home-garden scale, however, I have never felt the need. Call it my desire to rationalize, but I have since made a point of asking the great designers I have met in the course of my work how finely they plan on paper. Guess what? Many of them don't map it all out, either. They know something that beginning and overly cautious gardeners may not:

Most important to record are bloom dates (the start and finish of each plant); here's where you'll learn what flowers with what and hence learn to make good plant combinations.

gardens are often best worked out on the ground, by moving plants around again and again as the plants grow and cause the answers to the puzzle to reveal themselves. But even the loosest and most confident of all do plan, if less formally.

At the very minimum, make a list of the plants you wish to grow, and note how tall and wide they are, when they bloom, and what else they have going for them (good foliage, seed heads or berries later on, attractive bark, interesting winter structure, etc.). This is how I try to think of every plant—not just characterizing it by its flower color. To do so would be like thinking of a person as just a redhead or blond, rather than as a sum of all of his or her subtler qualities. It would also lead to a very dull garden, with most of the visual action centered in the spring instead of stretched out through the year—the way a lamentably large share of American gardens have been made.

Next make an informal chart, marking the months of the year across the top, left to right, and your chosen plants along the left-hand margin, top to bottom. Using the information about the plants you wrote down earlier, move across the monthly columns and put an X in each monthly box the particular plant should look good in. Then have a hard look at your impromptu chart: will this palette of plants give you interest through a long season? Identify the gaps—which will usually be every month except May and June, since that's when the most popular flowering plants do their thing. Research plants to fill them.

Other considerations: Looking at your notes, are there sufficient differences in heights, and in the texture, size, and color of the foliage of these plants to make things interesting? How do the flower colors that will overlap time-wise sound as a combination? Do the plants all enjoy the kind of site that you're intending for them (sun or shade, moist or dry, etc.)? Would the addition of bulbs (which take up very little room of their own) add to the season of this design?

Lilies, for example, could bolster July and August; winter aconite (*Eranthis hyemalis*), snowdrops (*Galanthus* species), and several other minor bulbs could start the proceedings as early as March, in the best of springs for me. Late-blooming bulbs such as autumn crocus (*Colchicum* species) would add a splash in September.

Another tip: Never attempt to fill in every last square inch of the design with permanent elements. Figure in some blank space, for annuals (whether the traditional flowering bedding plants, a tepee of three or four poles trained with annual vines such as morning glories, tender bulbs like *Acidanthera* or *Eucomis,* or tropical foliage fillers such as *Alternanthera* or variegated- and red-leaved *Canna*). The best gardens are loose enough to let things happen—whether by the gardener's impulse or by the garden's own spirit of self-expression.

That's the other rationalization that frees me from planning every inch of a flower garden on paper: the plants themselves. Many of my favorites—

Clary sage, or *Salvia sclarea,* seeds itself where it likes, in this case with *Rosa rubrifolia* and *Linaria purpurea.*

like clary sage (*Salvia sclarea*), tall verbena (*Verbena bonariensis*), larkspur (*Consolida ambigua*), and corydalis (*Corydalis lutea*)—won't stay where you put them anyhow, and have the habit instead of sowing themselves around here and there from year to year. (See "Editing Self-Sowns," page 74.) So I expect I'll go on putting them where the spirit moves me awhile longer, without a blueprint, and see what the garden has in mind for me.

JOURNAL MAKING

Another great source of free gardening lessons is your own adventures. Write them down, and learn from them.

A garden journal is usually a sturdy notebook, but a computer is a fine place to store garden records, too, though far less romantic. It will never become dog-eared by so many muddy fingers, or grow too wide to close because of all the flowers and leaves pressed inside. And you are less likely to have it with you when the great idea strikes. The critical thing is to create a system and use it.

Most important to record are bloom dates (the start *and* finish of each plant); here's where you'll learn what flowers with what and hence learn to make good plant combinations. Planting dates and the precise names of what you planted will be useful, and I think the exercise of writing them down helps them find their way into memory. Note where you got each plant and where it was placed. This latter detail will be especially helpful when you find yet another label in the middle of the lawn, or in the compost.

The garden journal has something no other book will: highly localized cultural information, geared precisely to your garden. Here is where we learn what is and is not possible, if only we write it down.

I like to record the arrival of birds and butterflies as they correspond with certain plants or aspects of my garden, which is how I realized that the hummingbirds always return right at the moment that the bleeding hearts (*Dicentra spectabilis*) open and that

they'll gladly keep sipping right through the last *Salvia* of the season. The increase in dragonflies and damselflies was astonishing one year, and then I figured out, after researching in the field guides, what had happened: we'd installed a water garden, and a bit of water to breed in is their dream come true.

I also have a page each month for self-criticism of a sort, a multicolumn chart whose categories simply read "Rescue," "Remove," and "Ugh!" The plants under the first heading are judged as worthy; they deserve a better home than I had given them. Usually some aggressive neighbor is crowding them out or they're getting too much or too little of something (light, moisture, *space*). The "Remove" list is not so clear; will I dig it out and compost it, or find the plant a new home in my yard or someone else's? The "Ugh!" list is obvious. Here's where I put the combinations that are more fingernails-on-a-blackboard than symphonies, or even improvisational jazz, which is a fine gardening style, too.

All this said, there's one problem: you'll get so swept up in sowing and weeding and edging and dividing (hopefully) that you'll forget. I'm conscientious about record-keeping in the down times, but by mid-May I begin to lapse. The answer: a point-and-shoot camera. Promise yourself to do at least this much in the way of record-keeping: take one roll of pictures every one to two weeks (more often in spring, when much is happening, less often as the rate of changes slows). Label the prints as to the date, and file them in an index-card file box with monthly dividers, an instant garden journal. I especially like to snip bits of plants from around the yard that would look great together, as a reminder of future combinations to create by transplanting. Some examples, recorded through the season, follow on the photographs on the next pages.

A large-flowered white clematis; the small, creamy flowers of *Clematis recta*; the pinkish white blooms of *Valeriana officinalis*; and wands of creamy green *Aruncus dioicus* coincide in early summer.

JUNE *2 kinds of clematis, aruncus, valerian*

COLOR NOTES BY MONTH

APRIL *goutweed, archangel, artemisia*

MAY *bleeding hearts, epimedium, alchemilla leaf*

APRIL *epimedium, pulmonaria, bleeding heart*

MAY *rose glauca, peony, barberry*

JUNE *bouquet of columbine*

JUNE *antique iris and honeysuckle*

JULY *sedum, hosta, geranium, daylily*

AUGUST *artemisias and*
variegated morning glory leaf

SEPTEMBER *ajuga, heuchera, lamb's ear*

AUGUST *ornamental grass blades,*
verbascum, corydalis leaf

SEPTEMBER *variegated weigela, stachys*

SEPTEMBER *blooming rosemary*
and pulmonaria

OCTOBER *asters and heuchera*

OCTOBER *dogwood, maple*
and magnolia seed pods

ZONES

I suppose it's essential to know the USDA Hardiness Zone you garden in, but there is a limit to how much you can rely on this fact alone to determine what you can and cannot grow. Forget about numbers and instead let the garden tell you.

My garden is technically situated in Zone 5a, which means it gets down to about −15 to −20 degrees Fahrenheit in winter. According to many of the books on perennials, then, I can't grow *Crambe cordifolia* or *Geranium renardii*, which are usually rated Zone 6 (cold-tolerant to only 10 degrees warmer than my typical winter, if any such thing exists). I certainly cannot grow *Aeonium arboreum* 'Schwarzkopf', hardy only to Zone 9.

As you may have guessed, all three live with me and have for years. Admittedly, the *Aeonium* (a succulent creature like a long-stemmed hen-and-chick, with the darkest maroon leaves) is in a pot. It is a houseplant in winter and an outdoor creature in summer; I brought it home from a California nursery, where conventional logic dictates a Zone 5 gardener should not have been shopping.

The geranium and the crambe tough it out in the cold all year round, despite what it says in the books. In the case of the crambe, it's never been a mainstay of American gardens, so its incorrect hardiness rating is probably just because not enough data were available on growing it in the coldest spots. In June, when it sends up its 5-foot by 5-foot cloud of tiny white flowers, like a gargantuan baby's breath, I'm glad I ordered it by mail and tried it anyway.

I killed my first plant of the geranium, and was set to believe the books and give up. But then I

Crambe cordifolia, in its second year in the ground, is already shaping up like a giant baby's breath.

thought about where I had placed it, which was a somewhat damp spot. I think wintertime moisture was the deciding factor in its death—I expect that the plant rotted. It's not just low mean temperature that affects a plant's survival in winter; it's also how good the drainage is, since so-called wet feet are particularly damaging then. Exposing them to wet winter feet makes it nearly impossible to grow the so-called Mediterranean plants—silvery artemisias, rosemary and lavender, ballota and such—all of which demand sharp drainage to survive the cold.

An aside: Conversely, dry shade is also one of the toughest places to grow things, and I have killed many plants in it. The ground cover *Epimedium* can take it, and so can certain ferns, somes sedges (*Carex* species), *Rodgersia podophylla* (which also loves the wet), and the white wood aster, *Aster divaricatus*—or at least those are the personal successes that come to mind. But even otherwise bone-hardy plants will give it up if asked to live without soil moisture. Don't confuse such losses with pure winterkill; if a plant is sited or cared for incorrectly, it may not make it even if it's technically two zones hardier than your climate.

Back to the main thought: Today geranium number two is happily growing in a base of sand between cracks in my fieldstone patio—not the kind of site the books say to give it, but because of the fast drainage there and thermal protection of the pavers, or so I speculate, it's just right in my supposedly "too-cold" zone.

There are other factors in the hardiness equation: whether there is snow cover when the deep freeze hits; how long ago the plant was installed (although even well-established specimens will kick the bucket in the worst of years); if the plant had a chance to properly "harden off" last fall. Usually the fall season is a gradual cooling-down phase for the plants, which slowly progress toward dormancy as days shorten and temperatures drop. If the first deep freeze comes very early, though, it may catch them unprepared and damage some tissue—a potentially costly event in shrubs and trees. Fertilizing too late can also doom a plant by causing it to send up succulent new growth that isn't ready for the stress of colder weather.

Repeat thaws before winter is really over can be a major killer, especially when they come in a tough month like January. Newly planted specimens are especially susceptible, because they aren't rooted in yet; even many bone-hardy plants will die if heaved out of the ground by freeze-thaw cycles.

Another major culprit: sunny late-winter days. Sure, it's a relief to us, but imagine standing out there in the bright sun all day and then, when darkness falls, having the temperature plummet to 40 degrees, or 30, or worse. Leaves, in particular, are susceptible, since they heat up to 10 to 20 degrees higher than the rest of the plant, meaning they feel the drop at night the worst of all. For broad-leaved evergreens (rhododendrons, for instance, or boxwood, or holly), particularly those in a sunny location, such chaotic weather means that leaves that may warm to 80 to 90 degrees by day (assuming it is about 60 to 70 out) drop 50 to 60 degrees at night if the temperature falls to 40 or 30—not a pretty picture at all.

This is when a lot of overwintered flower buds that are just starting to swell—ones on moptop hydrangeas (*Hydrangea macrophylla*), for instance, and the earliest-blooming magnolias—literally get nipped in the bud, too, and the gardener assumes that the plant isn't hardy, or at least its flowers aren't. Wrong, or at least maybe wrong. Plants sited on the southern side of a building are especially vulnerable to being awakened a little too early some years and then killed when a late frost follows unseasonably warm weather. It is great to have the first magnolia on the block to bloom, which the protected location yields, but in the years the weather is really up and down, you may have no flowers at all. The same plant on the north side of the building, out of the intense direct sun, would stay asleep a little longer, until the weather settled, and therefore miss the roller-coaster weather altogether.

My basic approach to zones: Never fear trying a plant that's one zone less hardy than your location. Don't buy 20 of something marginal as a test the first time out, though; that's too costly a wager. But do try a couple, preferably in different locations in the yard. Try again a second year. And if you fail twice but still covet the plant, pot one up and carry it indoors when the going gets rough.

Magnolia 'Ballerina' has fragrant waterlily-like blooms in early spring, before the leaves unfurl.

TAXONOMY LITE

It all sounds like *Plantus unknowniensis* at the start, but Latin is the mother tongue of gardening, and must be reckoned with. Besides being the only precise way of asking for what you want, it's often actually quite informative once you get the hang of it.

The genus name, which comes first, is expressed as Latin in an italicized word starting with an uppercase letter. A genus is a group of related species—*Aster,* for example. (The plural of *genus* is a surprise, by the way: *genera,* not *genuses.*) It is not always obvious what the genus name derives from, unless you speak Latin, know the history of botanical exploration, or possess some other equally arcane skills. Many genera are named for the explorer who discovered them (*Davidia,* for instance, after Père David) or for someone they were meant to honor (*Franklinia,* for Benjamin Franklin); others are simply Latin words for what they look like (*Aster,* for instance, means "star flower").

The species name, which follows the genus, is lowercase and expressed in italics. A species is a group of individuals that are related closely enough to interbreed (two distinct species in the same genus typically won't, with exceptions). Often the species name tells us something about the plant's background, such as where it comes from, or what color it is, or how it grows. Some species names also reflect their discoverer (*wilsonii,* for instance, or *sargentii*) or the person they were meant to honor, as do some genera, such as *Dahlia* (for a man named Dahl). Some that come up again and again include *virginiana* (of Virginia, or the area roughly equivalent to the early colonies), *occidentalis* (Western), *argentea* (silver), *aurea* (gold), *lanata* (fuzzy), *alba* (white), and *nana* (dwarf). Some are easier than others and even hint at their English translations, like *prostratus* and *horizontalis,* for "growing horizontally," and *decidua,* for "deciduous," or *variegata,* for "variegated." But don't get too excited too fast—memorization is the key to taxonomy, I'm afraid.

Sometimes the plant can be identified even more specifically, because it possesses slight differences from what is called the "straight," or normal, species. The third word in the name, if there is one, designates the cultivar (short for cultivated variety), meaning a version of the plant, generally an asexually propagated one (a clone), that is known only in cultivation (in gardening circles) and that was selected out of the average population of the species specially for some unusual feature, such as variegated leaves, different-colored flowers, or a weeping habit. This third word is usually expressed in English (roman letters) inside single quotes and begins with an uppercase letter.

A disheartening fact is that even for those who have been memorizing plant names for years, there is always more to learn. Blame the taxonomists who seem insistent on getting everything just right, down to the last chromosome, and keep reexamining plants under high-powered microscopes, pollen granule by pollen granule, and regrouping them. *Coleus,* for instance, is no longer *Coleus* but *Solenostemon;* perhaps the biggest shock of all was when *Chrysanthemum* ceased to be what we know it as (*Dendranthema* and other genera became the new home to *Chrysanthemum*'s former members). If you

But what you will be looking for when you shop for seeds, in person or by mail,

were hooked on their shorthand name, sorry, because mum's not the word anymore. But will I call them emas for short? I think not.

I believe it's important to know the taxonomically correct name, but as a gardener, being ever so precise can have its limitations. In catalogs, in reference books, and certainly in the aisles at the garden center, the renamed plants will probably still be where they were before the name change, and are likely to stay put for years. Don't try asking for a flat of *Solenostemon* just yet; stick with *Coleus*.

CHOOSING SEEDS
(OPEN-POLLINATED VS. HYBRIDS)

Seeds aren't any average mail-order product, since they're alive—and meant to stay that way for some time, even in inhospitable conditions like the Arctic tundra (where a certain kind of lupine germinated after sleeping, frozen, for 10,000 years) or in the decidedly warmer storage area of a Paris museum, from which seeds of a mimosa actually germinated after 221 years.

But what you will be looking for when you shop for seeds, in person or by mail, is not a guarantee of hundred- or thousand-year viability but the characteristics of the plant the particular seed promises to produce—attributes such as size, flower color, adaptability to a certain kind of climate, disease resistance, or some unusual feature of ornamentality (like red-stemmed 'Ruby' chard instead of plain green-and-white Swiss chard). Other times, it's some unexpected quality that breeders (through selection in favor of naturally occurring forms that they like more than others, or through active hybridizing work to try to force certain traits) have made possible, such as a bean that's easier to pick amid all those leaves. The purple-podded ones like 'Royal Burgundy', 'Blue Coco', or 'Trionfo Violetto' are pretty (though they don't stay purple when cooked), as well as easily seen. Cucumbers, too, can be elusive under all their foliage, but 'Little Leaf' has

what its name implies—and hence more obvious cukes. Dill would help make the cucumbers into good pickles, but in a small garden there's not room for 'Mammoth'. If you want seeds plus flowers and foliage, try scaled-down 'Bouquet'; if all you care about is lots of dill leaves, 'Dukat' (also known as 'Tetra') will serve you best. And so on.

These are the obvious factors to weigh when seed shopping. More complicated are the "political" aspects of buying seeds: whether to buy hybrids or heirlooms (open-pollinated kinds that have been around for 50 years or longer), and whether to buy treated or untreated seed only (certain seeds, particularly large ones like corn and peas, are presoaked in fungicide to prevent rot). The second choice is easier; if you want to avoid chemicals completely, buy only untreated seed.

I thought I was an open-pollinated person, in favor of plants that can be counted on to come true from seed each year, unlike hybrids, which may revert to the characteristics of one parent or the other and therefore aren't reliable sources of homegrown seed. I like the idea of buying a packet of seed for an heir-

---

is not a guarantee of hundred- or thousand-year viability but the characteristics of the plant the particular seed promises to produce.

loom tomato, then using the seeds of a single fruit from this year's crop to grow next year's whole crop, with enough seeds left to share with friends. The spirit of independence it fosters appeals to me.

When there's a good option, I'll pick the old-fashioned kind. I "vote" this way for sentimental reasons and also as a nod to helping preserve the plant's genetic imprint into the future, the way that other gardeners have before me because it was their great-great-grandfather's hand-me-down bean or the squash the Native American tribe in their region cherished. If you read the catalog descriptions and look at pictures of some of these old-fashioned types, you'll probably be won over, too.

These oldies are rarely the stuff of agribusiness, though—they're not tomatoes that can be picked green and shipped in trailers, baseball-hard, to ripen on a windowsill, or not at all. Since the heirlooms will probably never make their way into commercial production, individual gardeners have every reason to come to their support and grow them so they stay around, if only in small numbers.

But hybrids have saved me in more than one tough season in my gardening career, and I am thankful for them. If you have ever had an outbreak of blight in the tomato patch, a fungal infection that causes the plants to lose their leaves from the bottom up until they are nothing but a skeleton, or verticillium wilt, which can afflict susceptible varieties during a cold, wet season, you will sympathize with my temporary betrayal. Tomatoes are one of many examples where hybridization has yielded really useful plants, in this case because of their greater disease resistance. I am not so enamored of things like large-flowered dwarf marigolds, though—grotesque gold softballs on a 1-foot stem—or many of the other "space-saver" flowers that look out of proportion to my eye.

An heirloom tomato of pink flesh—and gargantuan girth.

GERMINATION TESTING

Germination testing of leftover seeds would make a good science project for grade-school kids, and it can delight and inform big people, too. If you can count to 10, you can test last year's seeds for viability, before wasting money on unnecessary replacements. Most are viable for three to five years, but there are exceptions.

Gather a couple of zipper-lock plastic bags, sheets of paper towel (one per variety being tested), small plastic labels, and an indelible marker. Count out 10 seeds of each kind being tested, place them in a row on a damp paper towel, and roll it up, with the label marked with the variety name rolled inside, too. Put the whole thing in a plastic bag (you can put a number of these rolls into one large bag), and leave it in a warm place. Check it after a few days, and again after a week, and so on, and make certain things stay moist inside. Count the seeds that have germinated, and multiply that number by 10 to get the percentage of viability. If eight seeds are alive, your packet is approximately 80 percent viable; go ahead and use it. If only three germinated, you may wish to reorder—or sow very heavily if you have a lot of seeds left or need only a few plants.

Some people like to wait till later on, close to outdoor planting time, to do their germination tests, particularly with the large seeds such as peas and beans. The ones that sprout are then used right in the garden, so the germination test doubles as a pre-sprouting process, speeding things along and reducing the chance of failure in cold springtime soil.

Even if your budget is large, try the foregoing experiment. There is nothing quite so extraordinary, or so humbling, as the sight of a cotyledon pushing out of a seed—a botanical baby being born.

THE YEAR'S FIRST SEEDS

It is too early to sow tomatoes, but not leeks—the official first seed of the vegetable-gardening season. Like onions, they can be sown indoors now under

Sugar Ann Peas

Bush Beans

Leftover seeds of peas and beans being tested for germination rate in late winter.

lights, because both of these botanical cousins require about 10 weeks' growing time before they go out in the garden approximately 4 weeks before final frost. In my zone I count back 10 weeks plus 4 weeks from about June (when hard frosts are uncommon), meaning that sometime in February is my seed-starting date for these crops. Each leek gets roughly a square inch of growing space indoors; if I'm feeling patient, I put a couple of seeds per cell in a partitioned flat, then thin to the strongest one per cell later. If I'm not, I sow a lot of seeds in a plastic flowerpot, then prick them off (separate them into individual growing spaces) by knocking the mass out onto the potting bench when the seedlings are several inches tall and teasing them apart to pot up.

Before sowing anything, though, I arrange my seed packets (leftovers and new ones) chronologically, according to the date they are to be sown—whether indoors or out. This is easiest if you mark the date(s) on the packet first; for instance, on a zucchini packet I would mark 5/15 and 6/30 for my zone; on a tomato, pepper, or eggplant packet, 4/15; on lettuce, "weekly from 4/1 to 8/15" (see "Starting Seeds," chapter 2, for details). With packets that require more than one sowing, replace them in the lineup after each use according to their next date.

FRUIT-TREE PRUNING: SHAPING THE FUTURE

Even in the Northeast, in the cold end of Zone 5 where I garden, winter offers up a few bright days, usually around early January, when the days are beginning to lengthen. We call this time the January Thaws, when it's sunny enough to go outside and do some pruning.

Today dwarf varieties of apples and other fruit trees are the standard, but when the half-dozen or so apple trees that remain from the old orchard I now garden in were planted, the norm was full-size trees. Their shapes were barely visible when I bought the property, overgrown with a combination of their own unnecessary, thicketlike growth and miles of multiflora roses and grapevines. Over a course of three years, the trees were brought back to some state of civility. This required aggressively employing two basic methods, which you, too, can use to improve the shape and yield of an overgrown fruit tree.

First, each and every year, remove all the water sprouts or suckers—thin, whiplike wood that juts straight up from the main limbs but could never support any fruit—with a folding saw or pruning shears, by cutting down to the supporting branch and leaving behind no trace of the sucker or its swollen base.

Then there's the harder part: taking out big branches. Step back and evaluate the tree, or even better take pictures. Have duplicate prints made up and draw on one set, blacking out the branches you think the tree would eventually be better without. How does it look?

The basic idea is to open the center of the tree up from the congestion too many branches create, which prevents light and air circulation from getting in there, and also to lower the crown if possible. Never remove more than one-third of the tree's live wood in any year; it will take at least three years, therefore, to accomplish what you imagined when you "pruned" the expendable parts of the tree out of the snapshot. Start by taking out dead and damaged wood, then any crossed or rubbing branches (remove the weaker or less well placed one).

When removing large branches, first reduce the weight of the limb by cutting off half of it. Pruning is a three-step process, to prevent tearing. The first cut

Before sowing anything, though, I arrange my seed packets (leftovers and new ones) chronologically, according to the date they are to be sown—whether indoors or out.

is always an undercut, made no more than halfway through the branch from underneath. Next, an uppercut, from the top, just slightly farther out on the limb from the undercut, will leave a stepped-off stub. If the limb is still very heavy and long, repeat the first two steps until you have still less weight. Then begin the final cut near the trunk, a one-step cut from above or below, depending on what angle suits the tree best. Make this just outside the branch-bark collar or ridge, which on many trees is a visibly raised spot where trunk and limb tissue meet. Never cut into the collar; but never leave a big stub, either. The tree will heal itself without wound paint; just leave the collar intact.

WITCH HAZELS

I have often said that if garden centers were open in February, witch hazels would be more popular than forsythia. What else is brave enough to bloom—with fragrant flowers, no less—when it is still winter outside? The native American witch hazel, *Hamamelis virginiana,* blooms at another odd time, in fall, and that's the one the popular astringent is made from. But the Asian species *H. mollis* (from China) and *H. japonica* (from Japan) have been interbred to produce some of the best early-blooming witch hazels, called *H. × intermedia,* and they include the varieties 'Arnold Promise' (large yellow flowers and yellow fall foliage), 'Diane' (carmine flowers), and 'Jelena' or 'Copper Beauty' (coppery orange flowers). The last three have orange-red fall leaf color; all have nice leaves during the growing season, too. Another desirable variety, 'Ruby Glow', has red flowers and orange-red leaves in fall; 'Sunburst' (yellow) is extra-early, but scentless.

In Japanese, the witch hazel is known as *mansaku,* or "first-flowering," and when the event occurs on a mature specimen it can be quite astonishing. Each individual flower is actually more like a cluster of tiny crepe-paper streamers or ribbons, which unfurl along the leafless stems when the late-winter days are even a little bit welcoming. Witch hazels, which are multistemmed shrubs and can reach from 6 to 15 or 20 feet high and wide, depending on the kind, are easy to care for, though somewhat slow-growing and difficult to propagate, and are therefore a bit on the expensive side among shrubs but well worth the money (and the wait). Often wood from the desired Asian species is grafted onto the more vigorous rootstock of *H. virginiana,* and from personal experience I can say be careful with this kind of plant. If branches start to sprout from the base of the rootstock, they will quickly take over and create a misshapen plant. Place your witch hazel in a partly sunny to partly shaded spot where the soil is rich in organic matter, moist, and a bit on the acidic side.

LEFT **One of the cleaned-up old apple trees, caught in an early snowstorm.** RIGHT **Hybrid Asian witch hazels.**

HELLEBORES

Why wait for the first of the bulbs or an extra-eager perennial like *Pulmonaria* to see some color outside? Even more understanding of the gardener's desperation for some hint of color in the late-winter landscape, before it's even earliest spring, is the hellebore, a longtime favorite among English gardeners and beginning to be known in America lately, too. No wonder, since many species are adaptable to shade, have evergreen foliage, and bear long-lasting flowers that may appear from late winter through spring, depending on which one you grow.

The earliest is probably the so-called Christmas rose, *Helleborus niger,* whose large, white waxy flowers are like single-flowered white roses, or camellias, with prominent yellow stamens. They may turn up during the holiday season in temperate England, and even in my frigid garden they're often trying to bloom through a crust of snow in March some years, even earlier in New York City and thereabouts. Unlike most hellebores, which will adapt to acidic soil if asked to, *H. niger* likes a dose of lime each year. Like those of most of the hellebores, its leaves are basically evergreen, though I like to cut off the tattered older ones as winter ends, which also serves to show off the flowers. (Even if I do not, the first hungry bees of the year will find them, and have a drink.)

Probably the most popular hellebores are hybrids of *H. orientalis,* the Lenten rose, with 2- to 3-inch blossoms variously shaped like bowls to stars. They range in color from white and cream through pinks,

mauve, wine, and darkest purple, and once a colony gets going in your yard, there will be every permutation of shape and color, including flowers with speckles and spots, as the blooms gleefully hybridize with one another. A mature plant, about 1½ feet tall, can bear 75 flowers or so, which is quite a show in late winter.

Because the foliage is evergreen, the hellebore makes an excellent ground cover in the shade of a woodland garden. It is also adaptable to some sun (don't bake it in the midsummer afternoon heat; pick a location that spares it that). I have seen *H. orientalis* blooming in Zone 6 as early as mid-February, before anything else on ground level, and even before the flowering shrubs and trees get going. Added to the winter cutting-garden scheme (see page 161), they are unrivaled. Cut only flowers that are well opened, since they do not continue to develop well indoors. A cool room will suit them better all around.

Several other hellebores have especially long-lasting chartreuse flowers and are as easy to grow as *H. orientalis.* Sun-loving *H. argutifolius* (sometimes seen in listings as *H. corsicus*) has blue-green evergreen foliage with sharp teeth. *H. foetidus,* native to England and Europe, has finely divided leaves like a palm frond. It will grow in sun or shade.

Almost every season, I notice "new" listings among the hellebores in smart catalogs that carry these worthy plants. That's because some hellebore species are closely related enough that they can be crossed with one another, and the hybrids that have resulted (such as *H.* × *sternii,* a sun-tolerant one, and *H. nigercors*) should be watched for as they become more widely available and prices drop.

Hellebores from nursery pots can be transplanted in spring or fall. First prepare the bed well, adding lots of humus-rich material (see "Soil Preparation," page 53), because these plants are meant to stay put for years. Mulch with fine-textured wood chips once the plants, spaced about 3 feet apart, are settled in. Each spring, if you're feeling generous, give each plant a trowelful of composted manure and a dash of lime. The only other chore is a bit of grooming when the foliage looks tired, but even without the tweaking they are a welcome sight.

LEFT ***Helleborus niger,* the Christmas rose, doesn't bloom until late winter.** RIGHT **Ornamental grasses in the snowy upper meadow are still handsome.**

PLANTS WITH STRUCTURE

Looking good naked is a challenge to people and plants alike. The plants that manage to do so are especially appreciated at this difficult time of year. I try to take at least one wintertime walk at an arboretum or public garden each year and add to my wish list of plants with good bare bones.

Garden books all cite the same plant as being synonymous with "good structure" and "winter interest": the contorted filbert, *Corylus avellana* 'Contorta', also known as Harry Lauder's walking stick. It is a twisted and wild thing, but by no means the only possibility. The contorted mulberry, *Morus australis* 'Unryo', is a larger-scale, faster-growing small tree with a corkscrew pattern when leafless. It is also easier on the pocketbook than the filbert, since it is easy to propagate and more vigorous.

Figure in some birches, too, with their white and pinkish copper trunks, and also some magnolias and beeches—though with the latter you'll have to pay a lot or wait a long time for the payoff, since beeches are very slow-growing, or at least don't develop the "bones" you'll want until they are many years old. Magnolias are a little quicker to comply; I bought my Loebner magnolia (*Magnolia* × *loebneri*) called 'Ballerina' for its fragrant, white water-lily-like flowers that come before the leaves open in early spring. It also proved to have nice structure and attractive gray bark, as does 'Merrill', a close cousin.

So do vastly different plants such as the shrubby fancy twig willows—*Salix alba* 'Chermesina', for instance, with its glowing stems in winter, an attention-getting mix of tan, rose, and apricot tones. Other shrubs have showy winter twigs, like the gold- and red-stemmed dogwoods (*Cornus alba*, the Tatarian dogwood, which has red stems, and *C. sericea*, with its red or golden twigs). If you cut back the older stems to about 6 to 12 inches in late winter each year, the vividly colored younger stems will show off to their best advantage. Another twiggy

An ancient lilac displays its great structure year-round. In fall, white wood asters clothe its feet.

shrub with winter interest is the ghost bramble (*Rubus cockburnianus*), which has, as its common name suggests, ghostly white canes.

The Japanese maples (*Acer japonicum*) are beautiful all year long, including in the leafless winter months, as are a number of somewhat larger trees such as *Stewartia pseudocamellia* (with camellia-like blooms in July, hot-colored fall foliage, and camouflage-pattern bark all year) and the paperbark maple (*Acer griseum*), which has peeling skin of a lustrous cinnamon color. (For more winter-interest plants, see pages 158 and 159.)

Plants needn't be woody to make a point in winter, even in harsh climates. A group of hardy yuccas, for example, is astonishing in the snow—a kind of desert-meets-Arctic moment. Underplanted with a carpet of creeping cotoneaster or juniper, and punctuated with wheat-colored ornamental grasses (such as large *Miscanthus*, left standing all winter), they are high-impact, even in a blanket of snow.

Many people assume that a weeping form of a tree will have great structure, but too often the so-called weepers are high-grafted obscenities that look like upside-down mops. Don't expect bargains in these trees, or a quick return, since they take time to take shape. They are art forms, and typically costly, well worth buying from the best woody-plant nursery you can find nearby. Some good weepers include the crab apple *Malus* 'Red Jade', the cherry *Prunus subhirtella* 'Pendula', and weeping katsura (*Cercidiphyllum japonicum* 'Pendula').

With structurally interesting plants, placement is critical, because you probably won't be walking in the far reaches of the landscape in the dead of winter. Site them where they can be enjoyed from a cozy spot such as the breakfast table or along the route you must take from car to doorway no matter what the weather. Underplant them with the earliest blooming bulbs—snowdrops (*Galanthus* species), glory-of-the-snow (*Chionodoxa* species), and winter aconite (*Eranthis hyemalis*)—to maximize the vista.

I try to take at least one wintertime walk at an arboretum or public garden each year and add to my wish list of plants with good bare bones.

By the traditional calendar, thoughts of spring could have begun a month ago, but on Groundhog Day, my troubled mind always calls up memories of Fourth of July. Just the mention of anything groundhog, in fact—or the sight of the first one to awaken from his burrow in the back meadow around April—and those guilt-laden synapses of mine take me right to that Independence Day not long ago and an ill-advised display of underground fireworks.

I tried to off a groundhog with a smoke bomb.

There, I feel better now that I've shared it.

At that time, like many city people, I fought the way things are, or at least objected to it energetically. The first year in the country house, we fought everything, I recall, not just the groundhog (or woodchuck, as we knew him to be called). On the morning after a harsh snowstorm, for example, we tried to travel back to the city, and in this self-important misadventure learned a whole new meaning for the word *respect*. We fought the deer,

brassicas and lettuce.)

Tomatoes, peppers, and eggplants make up my second group to sow at this time of year, and I start them next. They each get six to eight weeks indoors before being transplanted to the garden around the time that all frost danger has subsided—at least

lumping scheme of mine, saying eggplants actually need a week longer indoors than tomatoes and go outdoors a week later, for instance. They are probably right, in the best of worlds. But since I began lumping things this way, the system has worked much

who for generations had eaten beneath the apple trees we now insisted were ours; the mice, who asked only a warm place—our bedroom wall—to raise their children. We fought the logic that says that moss, not flowers, grows on the north side of a

even one lettuce seedling to an unexpected April heat wave, or one potted plant when it baked on the radiator, should realize what that means: without a proper sequence of the passing seasons, without the "inconvenient" weather like rain and sleet and even snow, there would be no farming and no gar-

ABOVE **Heirloom corn seeds ready to be direct-sown in the garden.** RIGHT **A finch's progeny, not yet germinated, was sown in a young tree.**

even a dark basement can become a growing space with this kind of setup. The shelves must be wide enough to hold the trays you are using.

Temperature also affects how seedlings germinate and grow, and not surprisingly the heat-loving plants such as peppers, eggplants, and tomatoes do best when the temperature's warmer; the cool-season stuff does just fine a bit cooler. Plan to have your lights on 14 hours a day (a household plug-in timer, which costs under $10, is useful).

Although I used to think of seed starting as an opportunity to recycle yogurt cups and other possible containers, now I'm hooked on an idiot-proof system called APS (Accelerated Propagation System), from Gardener's Supply Company, because it waters itself. The reusable Styrofoam planter should last many years; it includes a well to hold water, which is set beneath the form made up of individual cells. There are trays of fewer large cells for plants like tomatoes; others, with many small cells, are for lettuce and such. A piece of thick fabric, called capillary matting, sits beneath the bottomless cells, one end of which hangs into the well of water below, sucking up moisture as the potting medium in the cells begins to dry out. With this system and the timer, seed starting can even be accomplished by real people who are gone for an occasional weekend or don't get home at the same time each day. It also allows weekend gardeners to start seeds at their out-of-town home, because all but the largest plants will have plenty of water to last from Sunday to Friday.

Always use fresh, sterile medium labeled for sowing seeds. Often these mixes will be labeled "soil-less," meaning they're made not of soil but of peat, vermiculite, perlite, and/or milled sphagnum. Many books say you can sterilize used potting soil for reuse by heating it in the oven, but once you have filled your kitchen with the aroma of it baking, you'll buy new. Use the recycled stuff for less vulnerable plants than seedlings, or recycle it into the compost.

I usually sow a couple of seeds in each cell,

more smoothly, and since no two weather years are alike—particularly no two springs—I expect there is a kind of balancing act going on outdoors anyhow.

The key to growing healthy transplants is light. No, a windowsill just won't do. Invest in a set of inexpensive shop lights at the home-building center and fluorescent tubes to go in them (special plant grow bulbs are a bit pricier than ordinary ones; if you use the typical hardware-store fare, get the ones marked daylight, since they are slightly more color-balanced than the cool-colored typical fluorescents).

The relationship of the plants and lights must be a close one—they should never be more than a few inches apart. This means that either the lamp or the seedlings have to move as the plants grow. Suspend the lights on hooks and chains, or plan to prop up the flats at first with several boards, removing one board at a time to accommodate growth. An old bookcase makes a great seed-starting setup, if shop lights are fitted underneath each shelf. It's about two-thirds cheaper to make one this way than to buy a metal plant stand in the mail-order catalogs, and

The relationship of the plants and lights must be a close one—they should never be more than a few inches apart.
This means that either the lamp or the seedlings have to move as the plants grow.

because not all of them will germinate (though most, in fact, do if the seed is fresh and the conditions are right). As the two emerge and get their first set of true leaves (not the unidentifiable first ones, called seed leaves, that basically all look the same, but the ones that start to have the character of the specific plant), use a pair of small scissors to snip off the weaker of the two right at the base. Pulling may dislodge the one you intend to keep.

However else you may diverge from your plan, always stick to the system of when to start what; don't jump the gun no matter how tired you are of winter. Bigger tomato plants aren't better; small, stout, bushy 4-inch seedlings or thereabouts are what you're aiming for, not ones that have been in their cells so long that they are trying to reach the light or start to flower.

SOIL PREPARATION

You can choose not to start your own seeds or to draw your own garden design. You can even order a predetermined collection of plants or seeds that come with a plan, a so-called instant garden. But one step that cannot be skipped is soil preparation.

When I began my gardens, whether the beds for vegetables or the ones for flowers and shrubs, I prepared well. First, I roughly turned the soil in each area to be planted to a depth equal at least to my shovel's head—about a foot. Deeper, something like 18 inches, is even more desirable, especially if you will be installing large woody plants at some point.

Next, I layered compost, leaf mold, and sand on top of the roughly cultivated soil, so the bed looked raised up, higher than ground level. My layers were very generous—you simply cannot include too much organic (which simply means formerly living) matter in your beds. A 6-inch layer, worked into the underlying soil you already turned once, is a bare minimum. Organic matter serves to improve soil texture and drainage and also add to the soil's moisture- and nutrient-holding ability. Some organic amendments

have their own fertility; certain composts, particularly those from animal manures, add nutrients, but their main use is not as fertilizer but as soil conditioners.

Peat moss used to be universally recommended as a soil conditioner, but I no longer use it. First of all, I have a giant supply of would-be compost from my own yard wastes, plus the horse and dairy farmers down the road. Second, I am uncertain how environmentally sensitive it is to be harvesting peat moss from bogs, mainly in Canada, because they take so many years to renew themselves. Third, it is expensive. If you live far from the farm, take advantage of the free organic matter to be had in town—go up and down the roads in fall and ask for your neighbors' bagged leaves, or inquire at the local recycling or landfill facility about programs that give away or sell leaf mold and other composted materials.

Back to the hard work: By the time I had improved a couple of beds, I knew what I wanted for Christmas that year (or preferably sooner). A tiller proved invaluable, though I don't use it as often as I did in the first years.

I also like to work in some long-term amendments, which serve as sources of valuable minerals for plants over time, since they break down slowly. Greensand (for micronutrients and a slow-release form of potassium), rock dusts (for phosphorus and trace minerals), and bonemeal (for calcium and phosphorus) are three of my favorites. Hopefully, recent fears about the safety of bonemeal will be proven wrong and I can go on using it. I follow the package directions for application rates.

Soil care is a continuing commitment by the gardener—not just a one-time event. If you want to keep using the soil, you have to care for it. Each spring I top-dress my beds just as the plants emerge and the soil starts to

LEFT **The vegetable garden at tulip time.** RIGHT **Fertilize narcissus (and other bulbs) when the foliage arises.**

warm, applying a thin layer (about an inch) of screened compost to each area, along with a dusting of all-natural organic fertilizer (a slow-release fertilizer made not from chemicals but from meals and dusts that are by-products of other industries—alfalfa meal, bonemeal, blood meal, etc.).

When the soil is really warm, after Memorial Day, I mulch the beds with an inch or two of my favorite mulch, composted stable bedding made of wood shavings that have been used to line horse stalls. These additions—the early pick-me-up of compost and fertilizer, and the later mulch—will gradually break down into the soil. By mulching with a fine-textured material like the composted stable bedding, instead of giant wood chips, I'm also doing one more good thing: encouraging earthworms, which really like life beneath that kind of material. And they in turn aerate the topsoil and leave behind their worm castings—the ultrarichest compost of all.

There is one more step to soil care, and that is what is known as green manure. This is a crop, usually a grass or legume (a rye, clover, or vetch, for instance), that is sown when an area of the garden is not in use, then turned under when it is still young. The idea is that the nitrogen-rich green matter will break down and further texturize the soil. What crop to sow, and when to sow it, is the trick: the crop you select must fit your region, climate, and timing. Bountiful Gardens, Johnny's Selected Seeds, and Ronniger's (see Sources) all have good lists of green-manure possibilities with information about which one will suit what purpose.

HARDENING OFF

Your babies, the seedlings you started indoors, can't just up and move out without a bit of planning. The process by which seedlings are acclimated to the outdoors gradually is called hardening off.

Many harsh elements can fell a youngster that goes out before it's ready: the sun is far more intense than the artificial lights; the wind can wilt a plant in no time; and extremes of temperature from day to night can cause havoc, too. Add in a few days between your sowing date indoors and your setout date to gradually strengthen the plant, first with a daytime on a porch or other protected spot, then with a daytime under the shade of a high tree, where it gets indirect light but no sun, and so on. Bring the plant in at night until the third or fourth day, then let it stay out all night before planting day arrives.

ROSE PRUNING

A rose is not a rose is not a rose, at least where pruning is concerned. You will need to know what kind of rose you're growing—and by that I mean which class, such as hybrid tea, or climber, or rambler, or shrub—to prune properly. Start by looking up your rose in a book devoted to roses to identify its class.

Here are general rules: Once they are established, hybrid tea, grandiflora, and floribunda roses should be pruned every year about the time that winter protection is removed, usually just around the final hard-frost date.

No matter which kind or age of rose, prune out dead, diseased, and damaged wood; any canes that are thinner than a pencil; winterkilled tips; and any canes that are turned inward or crossed in the center or too simply close together (take out the badly placed one of the crossed or tight pair).

Healthy, vigorous wood is generally distinguishable from its exterior color (fresh green or reddish, but not brown or gray) and definitely from its appearance inside, in the pith at the core of the stem. If a cut reveals brown in the pith, cut farther down until you hit healthy white or greenish tissue.

Older bushes will also benefit from having one or two of the oldest canes removed right to the ground. Then cut the canes that are left (preferably about four strong ones) back to about 2 feet (grandifloras) or 1 to 1½ feet (hybrid teas and floribundas). The height after pruning would be higher in warmer zones, where roses are far bigger than in the Northeast. To encourage a well-shaped bush, which looks like an urn with an open center, these final cuts should be

Ephemerals are plants that come and go in a relatively short time, made ¼ inch above a strong, outward-facing bud, not flat across the cane but at an angle of around 45 degrees so that the high end of the cut is on the outside of the cane. Many experts seal the cuts with glue (such as Elmer's) to keep out pests.

Some roses aren't pruned now at all (except to take out dead or damaged stuff). Ramblers, which bloom just once each year, are pruned only after they flower (late June, perhaps), at which time up to a third of the oldest canes should be cut out right to the base. Climbers are pruned differently—cut off about 6 inches from the tips after flowering, then wait until they're dormant and remove an old cane or two to the ground. Climbers and ramblers won't need pruning for their first few years in the garden, since they will take at least that long to develop.

Whether yours is a rose that needs pruning now or not, all of them wake up hungry. Satisfy that craving with some nutrients: ¼ cup of Epsom salts per bush, all-natural organic rose food according to label directions, and bonemeal, for example. Sprinkle it all around the plant a foot or so out from the main trunk, and water well. Then, once the plants are fully awake, I start using soluble fertilizer (dilute seaweed concentrate and fish emulsion) monthly through July.

EPHEMERALS

Ephemerals are plants that come and go in a relatively short time, making their time with us all the more precious. Like the times of our infancy and youth, they are particularly fleeting.

Many of the best-known and most coveted ephemerals are woodlanders in origin, like Virginia bluebells (*Mertensia virginica*), the various *Trillium* species, bloodroot (*Sanguinaria canadensis*), Dutchman's breeches (*Dicentra cucullaria*), and squirrel corn (*D. canadensis*). But every habitat has its temporary stars, including the prairie, which features shooting star (*Dodecatheon meadia*) and prairie smoke (*Geum triflorum*), among others.

What does this have to do with gardening? Knowing the ephemerals that would suit your type of

The wakerobin, *Trillium erectum,* is a native inhabitant of the garden, forming small colonies in the front yard seemingly at will.

garden—prairie types for a meadow garden, for instance, or woodlanders for the shady realms—can greatly increase the season of interest in your planting, since ephemerals kindly disappear and leave room for something else to show off. The key is to mark clearly where they reside, so as not to disturb them when they are gone missing.

Even the common bleeding heart (see "Fumitories," page 96) is ephemeral, at least in all but the coolest zones. In a cool, moist summer, if grown in shade, it will wait to die down until perhaps early August; in a wickedly hot, dry year, there's a 3-foot gap in the garden by July. Some gardeners view this disappearing act as a liability, but I say not so. Think of ephemerals as opportunity makers instead, and plant something that is glad to share the space.

PEAS

A gardening tradition that appeals to me says to plant peas outdoors on St. Patrick's Day, but the last couple of years that would have meant shoveling some snow. Still, the biggest mistake with peas is planting too late. After late April for me is getting

making their time with us all the more precious. Like the times of our infancy and youth, they are particularly fleeting.

very dangerous; a mere zone to the south of me, the second week of April is probably cutoff time. Otherwise you will get vines but no peas, because they simply hate the heat. This fact of life rates peas (and spinach, for similar reasons) a place at the top of the list of spring chores. Just as soon as I can get into the vegetable garden without ruining the soil because it is too wet, I cultivate the pea row (and the spinach row, too) and sow the seeds thickly.

The peas will need support from a fence or a trellis made from plastic netting or chicken wire stretched over a wooden frame or from pole to pole. I use my dibble, a T-shaped wooden hand tool with a pointed, metal business end, to make a rough grid of inch-deep holes—two or three holes wide, but staggered, as if there were large-scale graph paper on the ground and you were making a hole in the center of each box *and* at every corner of each box, too. This is wide enough if the peas are up against one side of a fence, which they will grab onto with their built-in tendrils, and a little human urging.

When planting peas to grow up both sides of a support, I make an even wider row, a shallow foot-wide trench, and scatter it with seeds, then backfill an inch or so of soil on top of them and firm. Then I put up a mesh support of some kind running like a divider down the middle, or "plant" a thick row of twiggy brush (of which you will have amassed plenty at no charge during winter cleanup) down the middle of the row of peas just after planting, to keep them "brushed up." A good bit of pea brush will be shaped like a bouquet, with numerous twigs a few feet long radiating off the thicker main stem (stick that part in the ground). Particularly with the shorter varieties of peas, it makes a backbone that is easy and charming in an old-fashioned way—recalling the days before vinyl-coated stakes and plastic netting.

I first coat the seeds in a yield enhancer called an inoculant, a friendly black powder full of beneficial microbes meant to help legumes such as peas and beans to get up and growing. A bag of it, enough for all the peas I plant in a year, costs a couple of dollars; use it up, since it does not store well. It can also be used on sweet peas and other legumes.

A space-saving idea: Plant your peas at the back of the bed or row where your tomatoes, peppers, or eggplants will go, assuming that's against a fence. By the time those heat lovers go into the ground (about Memorial Day in my zone), the peas will be well along their way, and even by harvest time, the later crops will not be big enough to prevent getting at the peas. The peas can even be grown up one side of the tomato cages, so long as the vines do not completely enclose them and block all the sun from the emerging tomatoes.

Rather than planting only one kind of pea, I divide my available areas among a number of kinds. I grow mostly 'Sugar Snap', the classic of edible-podded peas, but I devote about one-third as much space to a sugar pea with a shorter days-to-maturity rating to stagger the harvest about a week earlier. A shelling pea like 'Tall Telephone' (also called 'Alderman') or its improved form called 'Multistar' should get a lot of space if you want peas without their pods, and make some room for Chinese snow peas, too, for stir-frying.

When the peas come in, usually the Fourth of July for me, along with the first of the new potatoes, I pick them, and pick them, and pick them. Left too long between harvestings, the production will slow down and much will be lost.

HYDRANGEA PRUNING

People always ask me about their hydrangeas—particularly the big moptop kinds (*Hydrangea macrophylla*) that flower blue or pink depending, respectively, on whether your soil is more acidic or alkaline. They are frustrated by lack of flowers and wonder what they're doing wrong.

These popular hydrangeas are easy if you understand their way of living: they carry the coming year's flower buds over the winter on the former year's growth, a precarious system if the place they are planted is subjected to late frosts, an extra-deep winter freeze, or an unkind cut of the pruning shears in spring, which slices the would-be flowers right off (assuming they survived the winter in the first place). Prune them just after flowering (in late summer) by removing one-third of the older stems (that have already flowered) right to the ground. Leave the best-placed and sturdiest of this year's growth in place to develop flower buds, taking out any stems that are badly placed, twisted, or crossing inward where

they cannot develop properly.

Though these most-beloved hydrangeas technically are hardy to Zone 6, in many oddball winters, a windswept spot, or an extra-harsh spring, the flowers will be killed there, too, so who cares if the plant survives? I don't attempt them at all outside in my area, a zone or more too cold, but if I were desperate to have one (such as the more delicate-flowered lacecap types, or one with variegated foliage), I'd grow it in a pot and carry it over in suspended animation in a garage, where I'd check it every now and again and offer it a drink if it were really bone-dry. The idea is to simulate winter of a slightly milder kind—not to prevent freezing, but to freeze without the combined evil forces of wind and alternate sun and ice.

Instead, outdoors I grow all the rest of the available hydrangeas for my zone, and they have become the backbone of my garden in summer through latest fall. The other most common hydrangea, the peegee (*H. paniculata* 'Grandiflora'), is just the

opposite kind of creature: it flowers on new wood only. **1** It can be pruned as hard as you like anytime from its messy shape early spring until it begins to sprout new growth. It can be trained to a single trunk (or several stems wrapped into one main leader), like a small tree, and in this form is a classic of older homes in the Northeast.

If the plant was a desirable size last year, I just cut back to the same spots as I did before, removing a year's growth. **2** Sometimes I go further and I cut back an extra bit, either way always making my cuts just outside a node. **3** I also remove all last year's flower stems.

4 After pruning, the peegee stands naked awhile, then finally, around mid to late May for me, the buds begin to break from the nodes and the cycle begins anew.

In August the shrub's giant cone-shaped flower heads begin to expand and turn white with greenish tinges, and then as the late summer edges toward early fall, they begin to color up to an old-fashioned pink like

Grandma's powder puff and on to tan, if left to meet the frost. They can be cut and dried in a bucket or vase without water when they reach their pink phase, and they will last for many years in a dried wreath or arrangement. Strip off the foliage before drying.

You may notice a difference in size of the flower heads among various specimens of this hydrangea, and that is largely affected by how it was pruned. If you cut it back hard, you'll generally get fewer but larger flower heads; if the plant's become a twiggy thicket, it will make many smaller blooms. This is true of many plants but obvious with the peegee, whose last name ('Grandiflora') means "large-flowered."

The straight species it was selected from, plain old *H. paniculata,* is large-flowered, too, but not quite so overblown and fluffy. The way that the lacecap hydrangeas are daintier than their moptop counterparts, *H. paniculata* is much more refined than *H. paniculata* 'Grandiflora'. These airier hydrangea flowers are actually two kinds of flowers combined into one flower head: the larger, showy male kinds, which are sterile; and the tiny, tight little things that look like buds, which are the female blossoms. I like these boy-girl ones best of all.

I also try to grow *H. quercifolia,* the southern native oakleaf hydrangea, but not so successfully, I'm afraid. Because its loose,

large flowers are produced on old wood, its buds are always lost in the despair of my Zone 5 winters. But it has peeling bark like a cinnamon stick and oaklike leaves that turn a great red-purple-bronze in fall, and even grows in shade, so I keep trying to make it happy. A zone farther south, it would be one of my favorites.

I do much better with *H. arborescens* 'Annabelle', another native, which bears giant white snowball flowers in summer that fade to greenish and look great for what seems like months. It can be cut down as far as you like, as if it were an herbaceous perennial, or left taller and just cleaned up of any wintertime

damage and thinned of some of the oldest stems, and it will reach more than waist-high. The size of the plant is up to you and the pruning, but unless you manage to kill it, which I think is basically impossible, it will flower anyhow.

The other hydrangea in my repertory is the climbing one, *H. anomala petiolaris,* which takes a bit of time to settle in and then becomes quite a large feature trained up a building or tree or over a wall. It can reach 60 feet if left unchecked by pruning shears. Its white summertime flowers look something like the lacecap's. It needs no pruning except to keep it in bounds, which should be done just after flowering.

4

MAGNOLIAS

The only shame about magnolias is that so few varieties are widely grown. You will certainly have seen the overblown saucer kinds (*Magnolia × soulangiana*)—usually some lipstick shade of pink—and the smaller-flowered stars (*M. stellata,* borne on a shrubbier plant to match the flowers' scale). Even in my sleepy little town, they are common.

The magnolias, evolution-wise, are probably the oldest flowering plants on Earth. They are also long-time favorites of gardeners. The spring-blooming magnolias are masters of defiance, seemingly unafraid to unfurl their giant blossoms even in the early weeks of spring. They do so well before their leaves appear, which in plant-speak is called being precocious. The spring bloomers come from Asia, unlike the magnolias of America—*M. grandiflora,* the southern magnolia, and *M. virginiana,* the sweet bay magnolia—both of which bloom in summer up north, when their leaves are out. The former is evergreen; the latter is almost evergreen, at least in warmer climates.

The precocious Asians are the most extravagant of flowering trees, for both their bloom size and the profusion of flowers they produce and for the intense fragrances many of them transmit, from lemony to sweet. Many of them also have good winter structure and smooth gray bark, plus furry flower buds they carry all winter. They look like giant gray pussy willows and are particularly beautiful in late winter when they begin to swell as flowering time approaches.

Among the whites, *M. denudata,* the Yulan magnolia, is very highly rated—the most elegant white of all. It can reach about 35 feet wide and high, and each of its many flowers measures 6 to 7 inches in diameter. The oldest Asian magnolia in cultivation (since 1780), the Yulan is one of the parents of the saucer types. 'Wada's Memory', a 20-foot fragrant hybrid, is another good white, as is sweet-smelling 'Merrill',

LEFT **Magnolia 'Ballerina' as its blooms unfold.**
RIGHT **In good fall-color years, its leaves turn yellow before dropping, an uncommon trait in magnolias.**

one of the Loebner hybrids. The many-petaled flowers of 'Merrill' are pleasing, but it blooms a little too early for my last spring frosts, so instead I planted its close cousin 'Ballerina', another Loebner type, which flowers about 10 days later. It has done just fine. With white scillas or white muscari carpeting the ground beneath it, it looks as if a giant, puffy cloud has settled in to hover above a carpet of fresh snow. And with my 'Ballerina', I got a happy surprise: hot acid-yellow fall color in about half the years so far—not a common thing in magnolias, but very welcome when the fall weather allows.

Magnolias have thick, fleshy roots and resent rough handling, so if they are to be dug from a field, it must be done in spring to give the transplants time to recover and settle in before frost. Make clean cuts on any damaged roots so they can heal; left mangled, they weaken the plant and slow growth. Container-grown plants (whether magnolias or any others) will generally suffer less shock from root disturbance at transplant time, but if it's a good-size specimen you crave, it won't come in a plastic pot.

With some exceptionally fast growers, like 'Elizabeth', a yellow-flowered selection from the Brooklyn Botanic Garden's breeding program, and one of a number of beautiful yellow forms. With others, it's excruciating to wait, although magnolias are known for being good bloomers even when quite young (which can be a strange sight, like a little girl in Mommy's oversize party clothes).

Give them sun, enough room to stretch out (they are often as wide as they are tall), and good soil that drains well but holds sufficient moisture for the plants to have a drink before it drains away, and they will be happy for years and years. I cannot recall having had to do any major pruning with my specimen of 'Ballerina', now about 15 feet tall, except to clean up bits of winter's damage—an easy garden plant indeed.

Corylopsis spicata **makes a good forsythia alternative, and looks good all growing season.**

FORSYTHIA ALTERNATIVES

Having complained for years about forsythia (except the little-grown golden-leaved form, which is far worthier than its boring green cousin), I thought it time to offer alternatives. I have already praised the early witch hazels (see page 41), but there are more possibilities. Winter hazel, or *Corylopsis,* is one fine example, a close relative of witch hazel, and there are several species, each bearing dangling chains of yellow flowers in early spring, before the leaves unfold. When these shrubs are underplanted with a mass of tiny blue bulbs chosen to coincide in bloom time, the effect is especially pleasing.

There are a number of species to select from, including *C. glabrescens,* the hardiest of the lot, which can reach about 15 feet. Its pale yellow flowers are scented sweetly. *C. spicata* (which in my Zone 5 garden has about a 50-50 chance of flowering success, since late frosts are common) is smaller, and I appreciate its spreading shape—perhaps 6 to 10 feet high and just as wide. Another reason I like this one is for its leaves. They open with a pinkish purple tinge, then turn a particularly beautiful blue-green for summer, retaining a touch of pink at the twigs.

C. platypetala is another 15-footer; *C. pauciflora* is the little guy of the bunch, only 5 to 6 feet high and wide. Its foliage is also about half the scale of its larger brethren, and unlike the others, which prefer full sun, the latter is better off in light shade. Winter hazels may go a pleasing yellow in fall or just go brown; I haven't quite figured out which does what which year or why.

A couple of informal-looking shrubs, the native spicebush and the cornelian cherry, are also very valuable and are completely carefree. The former, technically known as *Lindera benzoin,* has tiny yellow flowers with a spicy fragrance in early spring and very good yellow fall color. Its small fruits are appreciated by birds. It can tolerate the shade of a deciduous woodland garden, where it fits right in. The latter, *Cornus mas,* is actually a kind of dogwood, not a cherry at all. But its large, glossy red fruits look like cherries—if you get over to see them before the wildlife has at the crop, which I rarely do. Grow *C. mas* for its very early, yellow flowers, like so many little yellow puffballs, that in their profusion over the 20-foot by 15-foot mature framework create a fantastic yellow haze. It also has attractive, peeling bark and can be pruned more like a small tree if desired, by cutting out some of its multiple stems. Give it a spot in the sun for best flowering and fruiting.

There is no jasmine scent to yellow-flowered *Jasminum nudiflorum,* but that's the only bad thing I have to say about it (except that it's too tender to bloom for me). A sprawling creature well suited to arching over a wall, it will put out bursts of bloom anytime the sun shines and the days begin to warm in late winter and earliest spring—a welcome sight.

Shadbush, or serviceberry (*Amelanchier* species), is not yellow-flowered but white. The smallest among this genus of native small trees is *A. canadensis,* which stays under about 15 feet; a friend has also shared with me a piece of what he knows as *A. stolonifera,* a much smaller, spreading thicket. All the serviceberries have clouds of delicate white blossoms, red (later black) fruit that's tasty (to birds and people), hot fall color, plus handsome gray bark.

I could go on with my forsythia alternatives: There's native *Fothergilla,* with white bottlebrush flowers, beautiful leaves, and fiery fall color. The various unusual pussy willows (*Salix* species)—ones with black catkins (*S. melanostachys*), or rosy ones, for instance *S. gracilistyla*—would be nice massed in a moist spot. If pink is more your taste, what about the deciduous pinkshell azalea, *Rhododendron vaseyi,* which blooms in a woodland setting before its leaves (or those on the trees around) unfurl?

Some favorites among the minor bulbs in other genera

ODD MINOR BULBS

I grow large-flowered tulips in my vegetable garden for cutting purposes (see page 85), but for the garden my tastes run to less formal flowers than these. The smaller tulips, often called botanicals or species types, are much more suited to designing with if your garden is looser in style or on a smaller scale. Another advantage is that some of the botanicals are extra-early, beginning in early April (even late March in slightly warmer spots than mine) in the case of *Tulipa pulchella violacea*, a 6-incher with violet flowers and yellow throats, or *T. turkestanica*, which grows about 8 to 10 inches high and produces clusters of starry white flowers with orange-yellow centers. *T. clusiana* (the peppermint-stick tulip, with flowers striped vertically in red and white) is another species of less imposing stature than the typical tulip, though a bit later than the other two. (Around late April, there are also some large-flowered but dwarf types—the Greigiis, with their red-splashed foliage and bold red, yellow, or orange flowers just 6 to 10 inches tall; and the Kaufmannianas, about 4 to 8 inches tall, with big flowers that may be white or in sunny colors, often with a contrasting center.)

Some favorites among the minor bulbs in other genera include *Chionodoxa sardensis,* a tiny, gentian blue flower that is so pleasantly unlike the yellows and other pastels of spring. It is harder to track down than *C. luciliae,* which is pale blue with a white throat, which does not interest me one bit as much, since it starts to look like so many other pale-colored spring bulbs. Winter aconite, *Eranthis hyemalis,* produces bright yellow buttercup flowers backed by an Elizabethan ruff of green and is also very early, as are the more familiar snowdrops. If you leave the faded blossoms to wither in place, all of these will sow themselves around (or somehow manage to end up where you did not plant them), and that is another facet of their charm.

The grape hyacinth (*Muscari armeniacum*), whether the classic dark blue or the white or paler

CLOCKWISE FROM TOP LEFT **Muscari, purple *Crocus*, botanical tulips, two other kinds of *Crocus* (striped and yellow ones), and *Chionodoxa* are some common minor bulbs.**

include Chionodoxa sardensis, *a tiny, gentian blue flower that is so pleasantly unlike the yellows and other pastels of spring.*

ABOVE **Take care when cleaning up winter debris from delicate shoots; sometimes only hands will do.**
OPPOSITE **An old birdhouse in an older apple tree.**

blue forms, and even the overblown violet cousin called feather hyacinth (*M. comosum* 'Plumosum') are always welcome, but they trick the gardener into a bit of a panic in fall when they begin to send up grassy leaves. This is no cause for worry; it's part of the muscari's lifestyle, not something that you, or the weather, has done wrong. Perhaps the most intricate concoction of all is *Fritillaria meleagris*, the checkered lily or guinea hen flower, which bears nodding bells of wine-purple or sometimes white, distinctively marked in checks. There is no more special spring bouquet than a few of these set in a tiny glass.

Small-flowered bulbs are easier to deal with in garden beds than their bigger cousins, because their foliage, which must remain on until it fades naturally, to replenish the bulb for next year, is less difficult to disguise. If planted among ferns, it is like magic: as the bulbs' flowers fade, the fern crosiers unroll and cover the area with a fresh green glade. Except for the tulips and crocus, which require more sun, these bulbs are fine in areas that will be shaded as the season progresses, so long as they get enough sun in spring to flower and ripen their foliage.

The small bulbs are best where you can see them, along the edge of a pathway or near the front of beds. Never plant bulbs sparingly, particularly not the little ones, since their best effect is one of large, amoeba-shaped drifts, not sparse polka dots or stripes. Generally speaking, plant small bulbs three times as deep as the bulb is wide, or so the tip when buried is about 2 to 3 inches below the surface; with the really tiny things I increase the depth a bit to reduce the likelihood of animals digging them up before they get established. Always site bulbs where the soil is good and drains well, since they are prone to rot in soggy spots. Some, like the *Eranthis*, are rather unbulblike (it's a tuber, technically, but looks more like a brown lump), and who knows which end is up? I have had success with them anyhow and am fairly certain I did not get every one exactly right in planting. Grecian windflowers (*Anemone blanda*) are the same way; I soak both in a dish of water the night before planting to help them get up and growing, and I keep the area watered while they settle in. Feed bulbs when the foliage starts to poke through the ground in spring, sprinkling an all-natural organic bulb fertilizer over the area where they are growing, according to package directions.

If not for the astonishing prices, I would have a show of smaller bulbs again in fall. I'd probably plant a thousand autumn crocuses . . . perhaps even in the lawn, and I'd mow the grass only until the *Colchicum* began to show signs of breaking through the soil. Even a small cluster is startling, probably because they look so much like spring.

NARCISSUS

The most accommodating of all bulbs are the *Narcissus,* which not only make themselves naturally unattractive to animal pests by being poisonous but also gladly multiply underground into bigger and bigger colonies over time. Each of the first five years I was in my house, I planted nearly a thousand of them, and today there is no regret about all the mud-stained knees and wet, cold fingers suffered.

Not only do narcissus boast great good looks, but the earliest-blooming varieties of narcissus (and other early bulbs) are useful as divining rods to find the microclimates in the landscape—spots where topography, protection of some kind, or unusual light conditions make things jump up extra early or hang back a few weeks. In my backyard (the south side of the house), the very same variety of daffodil blooms a week to 10 days earlier than it does out in front (the north).

To my eye (and nose) 'Thalia' is a must-have, bearing highly fragrant white blooms that are carried in groups. It is a Triandrus narcissus, and its clustered flowers are not so overblown as many daffodils are and therefore have a grace to go with their pristine color. I always scour the lists of catalogs like that from the Daffodil Mart for other fragrant offerings, since aroma is such a prize at this early time of the growing year. Place the best-scented narcissus near doorways and paths.

The pheasant's-eye type, or Poeticus narcissus, is another particular beauty and likewise highly fragrant. Its has flat white petals and a tiny, short golden cup at the center that is edged in red. The Tazetta, or Poetaz, varieties are also fragrant, and their flowers are often white, sometimes with a colored smallish cup. (The tender paperwhites we force indoors are technically Tazettas, but they are useless in most gardens and cannot be reforced.)

There are so many shapes and color combinations, from clusters of miniature powder puffs to classic yellow trumpets, it's a matter of taste. Whatever your visual pleasure, be certain to select from among the list for very early, early, midseason, late, and very late bloomers, so that you can enjoy drifts of narcissus for about two months.

Never plant them in small groups; a dozen is a minimum cluster, and 25 or 50 is better—or 100. I like them in giant waves beneath my apple trees, where their flowers and the apple blossoms overlap. I simply mow around the drifts until their foliage begins to wither, in July. I also planted large groups in the woods around the garden, beneath deciduous trees and shrubs. Although by summer the woodland floor will be deep in shade, before the leaves come out in spring there is plenty of light to allow the daffodils to bloom and even ripen their foliage. For long-distance views, plant large numbers and choose the less delicate varieties—large-cupped whites and yellows—that will read from a long way off.

Daffodils can be a nuisance in flower borders, because inevitably you will pierce some with a fork or spade when digging something in or out. I cannot resist, however, and have groups of them there, too, in clusters of about 15 to 20. When planting daffodils, forget the demure bulb planter, and just dig big trenches. Lift the turf carefully (if there is any), folding it back, and dig below to the proper depth (about 8 to 9 inches, so the bulbs' tips will be a good 6 inches underground). I lay them in the flat-bottomed trench, points up, and with about 6 to 8 inches between bulbs; backfill and fold the turf back; then water well. Under old trees like the apples, where roots present an obstacle, you may wish to rent an earth auger (electric- or gas-powered, like a small posthole digger) to make individual pockets for the bulbs beneath the canopy of the tree.

Bonemeal added to the trench or hole at planting time is a nice touch, but I am not so fussy when I am planting in the hundreds or thousands, and these stalwarts seem to thrive without the extra love.

LEFT **An old headboard, found in the woods by the house, serves as a rose trellis; daffodils bloom nearby.**

To my eye (and nose) 'Thalia' is a must-have, bearing highly fragrant white blooms that are carried in groups.

PULMONARIAS

Leave it to an asthmatic to fall in love with a plant named lungwort. And so I did, years ago, after the first bit of one was unceremoniously wrenched out of the ground by a nurseryman from his garden after I commented that I liked it very much.

"Have a piece," he said, and threw a plant, soil and all, into the back of my pickup, along with the properly potted-up things I'd purchased. "Just cut off all the leaves when you get it home, and water it in well."

Today I have dozens of plants of this unnamed, attractively spotted pulmonaria, along with six or eight properly named forms whose foliage ranges from plain medium green (*Pulmonaria rubra*) to nearly all white ('British Sterling') to a ghostly silvery green ('Margery Fish'). Some are narrow-leaved, like 'Roy Davidson' and the even narrower 'Bertram Anderson', which are particularly attractive. The cul-

tivars fall into different species, but just look for them by their varietal names. They are among the easiest and earliest of perennials, fine flowering ground covers for shady spots, where they will happily sow themselves around so you can share your own pulmonaria crop, too.

Pulmonaria got its unfortunate common name from 16th- and 17th-century herbalists, who tried it for treating lung ailments. Their rationale, reportedly, was that the spotted leaves looked like a diseased lung. I beg to differ; they are simply beautiful. The first one to bloom is *P. rubra*, which, as its name implies, is red-flowering—a very unusual color for early spring. It is so early that it is just the second perennial, after the hellebores, to bloom for me each year, continuing for many weeks until spring is well advanced.

Most of the pulmonarias are blue- or pink-flowered, although 'Sissinghurst White', for one, isn't. The little funnel-shaped blooms come before the leaves, or when just the scaled-down first crop of foliage shows. Later, cut off the fading flower stalks and the pulmonarias will form handsome clumps of foliage, mounding about a foot high and just as wide.

The only trouble occasionally encountered is a bit of powdery mildew, particularly when the plants are stressed early by lack of moisture, then exposed to the muggy days. Watering well all season will help prevent it, and so will planting where they have some breathing room. But if it sets in, simply shear the plants to the ground, water, and let them regrow. A thorough fall cleanup, removing all spent foliage, reduces the chance of overwintering mildew spores. This is the same treatment recommended for *Phlox paniculata* and for bee balm (*Monarda* species), similarly inclined to take a powder in difficult summers.

LEFT **The first pulmonaria to bloom, *P. rubra*.**
RIGHT **A stand of 'Thalia' narcissus (center) under the lilac in April, when the garden comes awake.**

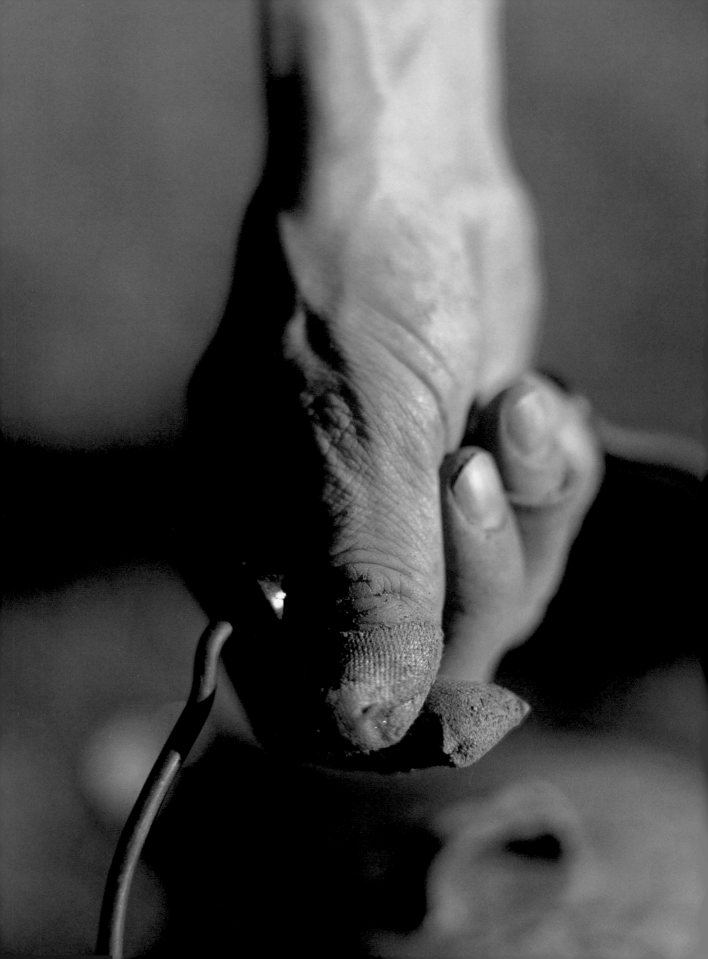

Youth

Like a graduating senior in that pointless last week of school, I have lost all ability to concentrate. I hadn't been sure, until I sat down to write this, exactly what was on my mind, but it is full, so very annoyingly full that I awaken every morning when it is still dark to the tape playing in my head. It is a droning, relentless list, with lots of static punctuating entry after entry of musts, to-do's, and did-I-remember-to's.

Probably it is partly the disease of gardening that does this to a person come June. At this time of year in my neighborhood, prime planting season is dwindling down to a precious few days, the only ones left before the merciless summer wilts all but the most vigorous transplant, and the most vigorous planter. This is my gardening prime, I suppose, as I toil away alone, peacefully, on these late-spring weekends. This thought does not console me this year, though, because on one of these Saturdays very soon, any day now, I'll turn 35 to the minute as I kneel to plant a hill of beans. With dirty nails and sunburned shoulders, I'll sit beside my hill of beans and smile, or cry, at what my passion has amounted to.

I have no progeny but my plants, and the birds and toads and furry creatures who are welcome nesters in my garden. Three pairs of tree swallows are raising graceful families within my view, and while I work, the mothers poke their pointed faces out of their birdhouses' holes and watch me suspiciously, never fully trusting that I am a friend. Or are they just amused at the kingdom I have created within the fence, or the fact that I built a fence at all? They are putting on a show for me, but despite the example of the birds, and the hassling from the people around me worried about my biological clock, I do not hear it ticking. The sound I hear is the gardening clock—its insidious alarm is the one sounding in my ear before every dawn.

Thirty-five probably isn't awful, except when I think about it the way I always do, like this: I have only 30 or so more summers to perfect my life's only handiwork—to start the sturdiest seedlings, to train tomatoes that stand tall, to coax perennials to coexist in pleasing combinations, to prune the perfect tree, to arrange a bowl of flowers just so, or to pickle or otherwise make use of my whole harvest, down to the last disfigured, knobby cuke.

I need more time.

Gardening is the story of life and death and life again, sometimes miraculously emerging from where no life seems possible, and it is also the story of the seasons in between those scary start and finish lines. Plants, like us people, want to live. Just when I think I have killed the santolina or the lavender in the herb plot, up they pop again from the base, twice as thick and bushy, as if from their own ashes. The aged apple that a storm sheared to half its girth refuses to give it up, and even promises fruit this year. A new-fangled, water-filled cloche fell smack on top of the tomato it was supposed to be protecting, but no matter, the thing is growing mightily anyhow. Miracles.

These warm days are times of horticultural and spiritual bounty, of first harvests and of promises in all the growing things. But they are going too fast to suit me now, and like the little toad who dug in beneath the baby heads of lettuce, I am trying to stand my ground against the stronger will of passing time. Like the lettuce and the toad, I am aging, and that is what I feel most these days.

To fight the forces, I am planting furiously, as many plants as I can place in the earth on each fair day. In went a berry patch, a second big perennial border, a separate bed for onions and garlic outside the protection of the vegetable-garden fence; and to soften the fence posts and wire, the contents of a dozen pots of flowering plants—rugosa roses, potentillas, caryopteris, buddleia—have made their way into the moist, soft ground outside.

An early June birthday is a sweet one in the garden, where clumps of perfumed peonies seem to open just for me. With some yellow roses and the last lilacs, they will make heavenly bouquets, but who will have the heart to pitch them when they're through? There are the first tiny sugar pea pods for the birthday dinner table—especially early this year—plus so much in the way of tender salad fixings, and there is still time before the spinach fades. And what flower is more beautiful than the purple globes above the chives, even if they do not smell so sweet?

The really hot days ahead will bring their own special gifts—truckloads of squashes and tomatoes and oh, so many beans—but these more durable vegetables have less appeal than early summer's specials. Because they grow so easily, no matter how we mistreat them, I do not hold them nearly as precious as their fleeting garden neighbors that last only a minute because they cannot take the heat. The asparagus, the peas, the peonies and lilacs—those are the ones we gardeners cherish in our memory as we approach the heat of summer, and in my midlife crisis I worry that I have already had half my share.

These warm days in the garden are times of horticultural and spiritual bounty, of first harvests
and like the little toad who dug

TRANSPLANTING Whether transplanting a large shrub or a tiny vegetable seedling, the most common, often fatal, mistake is failing to tease apart the root ball. When a new gardener transplants an acquisition from the garden center, he or she yanks at the top of the plant to get it out of the pot but treats the root system and attached soil like a newborn baby. In fact, a plant should never be dislodged from its container by pulling on the main stem or

leaves. Rather, you should bang the top rim of the pot sharply on a bench or table while straddling the plant's main stem between your fingers so it doesn't go flying onto the ground. With flexible containers, also push up from the bottom of the flat or cell-pack.

Always water plants that are set for transplanting before unpotting them—especially with large ones, do this at least a few hours or so beforehand, so they can soak up a good drink in order to combat the stress of leaving their childhood home. Once they are out of their pots, have a close look at the mass of roots and soil you have uncovered. Are the roots wrapped around the soil ball in exactly the shape of the container, and do more roots than soil show? The plant is root-bound, and merely popped into a hole as is, the roots may not grow out into the new soil but just stay tightly balled, which eventually chokes the life out of the plant. Self-strangulation is a very common cause of death in container-grown shrubs and trees, which unlike field-grown plants often become badly root-bound if left in their pots too long. Though container plants—the standard of the nursery industry today—are easy to work with, readily available, and typically undergo less transplant shock than field-dug plants, when they are even slightly root-bound they need a little bit of the gardener's help to thrive.

With young annuals and vegetables in small pots, I use my fingers to gently pull the roots loose and untangle them. Some of the soil will fall away, which

is fine; some roots will snap, too, which is unavoidable. With perennials, shrubs, or trees that are a thick, solid mass of roots, I am a bit more athletic and frequently use a knife or the point of my pruners to score the root mass top to bottom in several places around the ball and also to untangle the bottom of the mass. An exception: I look up or ask the nursery whether a plant is taprooted—having a long, main root—or for some other reason hates transplanting, and if so, I handle the plant in a much gentler fashion.

Another transplanting error that leads to poor performance, or disaster, is planting at the incorrect depth. A tomato or a marigold or a cosmos will be delighted to be buried up to its neck, because it has the ability to root off its stem all along the way. But a magnolia or a beech buried too deep will not thrive. In the least costly situations, as with peonies or bearded irises, too-deep planting will mean they never bloom. But many trees and shrubs will die, if not at first, then gradually over a few years. Look at the level the plant was at in the container (assuming the root ball was in good shape, and not eroded), and match it.

The usual discussions of transplanting focus more on the preparation of the hole than on any other step—whether to amend the soil before backfilling around the plant, whether to make a hole significantly larger than the root ball, and so forth. "A $10 hole for a $5 plant" was the prevailing logic for

and of promises in all the growing things. But they are going too fast to suit me now,
in beneath the baby heads of lettuce, I am trying to stand my ground against the stronger will of passing time.

ABOVE **An annual seedling is root-bound and must be teased apart with a finger before transplanting.**
OPPOSITE **A patch of self-sowns includes *Linaria* and *Verbascum*.**

years, but a change is in the wind. Whereas I once used heaps of peat moss for amending the soil excavated from the hole before backfilling, I have stopped. First, I don't buy peat anymore; second, it is illogical to give the root ball a foot, say, of lightened planting medium all the way around it, then once the roots get that far have them confront the harsh reality of the surrounding soil—clay, rocks, whatever.

As I said, my primary concern is the level, so I am careful not to put anything unstable, like clumps of sod or unfinished compost, into the bottom of the hole, which could settle. I use my hands and also a stick, whether half a bamboo cane in a smallish hole or a broom or shovel handle in larger ones, to prod around the edges and eliminate air pockets. I water once the plant is in place (some people water into the partially filled hole, then finish filling, but this creates a squishy, muddy mess). But I do this only after I've formed a ring of soil around the base of the filled-in plant, like a high-lipped saucer, to collect the runoff. This soil saucer is one of the old-fashioned transplanting techniques I still follow, for everything from tomato seedlings to roses to trees.

The other item under debate is whether to top-prune the plant to adjust for losses in root mass. Years ago, that was always recommended . . . but then, the standard plant was a field-dug one, balled and burlapped, not one grown all its life in a pot. Field-dug plants necessarily suffer root loss when excavated, but unless it is badly root-bound, a pot-grown plant may not. I evaluate the damage below and decide on a case-by-case basis whether to reduce the aboveground portion of the plant, and I also take the plant's growth rate into consideration. I'm less eager to cut one-third out of a slow-growing beech or a 'Blue Mist' fothergilla than I am to hack back a weedy creature like a willow.

Final tips: When woody plants suffer root damage in transplanting, always take a sharp pruner and recut major roots at the point of damage, so the ends are clean-cut, rather than torn or mangled. Regeneration is said to be easier this way. If your new transplants are destined for a sunny spot, plant them in the late afternoon so they will have most of a day to adjust before being fried. Keep them well watered, and offer a temporary bit of shade by draping a piece of Reemay (see page 162) propped on stakes or right on the plants.

EDITING SELF-SOWNS

Most people approach gardening as a form of addition: you add more plants until you like what you see. But there is also a lot of subtraction to the process, particularly with certain annuals, biennials, and short-lived perennials that tend to sow themselves about if allowed to go to seed. The best gardeners learn to identify their self-sowns each spring (which may not show until quite late) and work around them, or at least some of them, since the crop will usually be overabundant and must be thinned.

Gardening by reduction, as this process is called, means you cannot compulsively clean up every last

scrap of evidence of last year's garden before frost or cultivate every last bed before spring even arrives. Excessive tidiness or too-early and aggressive spring-time cultivation and mulching will squander a great resource—the progeny of your own garden, sown where the plants themselves think they should grow and always more spontaneously spaced than the gardener's hand could dictate. Some extras (except untransplantables like annual poppies) can be relocated when the seedlings are a few inches high.

What will self-sow is not consistent from place to place; forgiving climates probably have more candidates than do harsh ones. But generally speaking these worthwhile and generous souls can be counted on to do it: *Cosmos, Cleome, Perilla frutescens, Verbena bonariensis,* clary sage (*Salvia sclarea*), purple orach (*Atriplex hortensis*), purple amaranth, opium poppy and other annual poppies, *Nicotiana,* sweet alyssum, *Scabiosa,* toadflax (*Linaria purpurea*), mullein, larkspur, *Angelica gigas, Portulaca,* copper fennel, and dill. (Tomatoes will, too, but I assume you won't be happy about that from a design standpoint.)

I learned about self-sowns one spring years ago, when the shortest route across the lawn to the compost pile was suddenly turning purple. Apparently on the way to the compost heap, I'd dropped something—perilla seeds, to be specific. Like following a Hansel and Gretel trail of bread crumbs, I could trace the paths I'd taken on my cleanup rounds the previous fall. Now I know to leave a few of each plant standing to do the job, and I also use pulled-up, seed-laden plants as a source of seed for other areas of the garden, where I shake them before composting the remains.

Self-sowns have an inclination to spill into gravel paths and driveways and into cracks between paving stones, where the extra warmth and drainage suits them. Tall things may choose to march to the front of

Eager self-sowers include (clockwise from above left) *Verbascum, Cleome, Angelica gigas, Linaria purpurea.*

the border as if to say to the gardener "don't follow the rule of small at the front and large at the back so strictly!" I have come to cherish their resurrections, and their insurrections, too.

TOMATO, PEPPER, AND EGGPLANT SECRETS
No vegetable is more commonly homegrown than the tomato (*Lycopersicon lycopersicum*). There are enough varieties to choose from for a lifetime of taste tests, with hundreds of named kinds available in specialty catalogs such as that from the Tomato Growers Supply Company (see Sources). Don't just settle for what the garden center propagates.

Although 'Sweet 100' and its later sibling 'Sweet Million' probably dominate the cherry-tomato market, even among these little tomatoes there are outstanding alternatives: 'Chadwick's Cherry', carried by Bountiful Gardens (see Sources), is an ample, golf-ball size with good tomato taste; 'Sungold' is tangerine-orange and very tasty. For novelty in a salad tomato, try 'Black Prince' (mahogany brown and juicy inside) or pink-fleshed 'Oxheart'. There are better paste tomatoes than the standard 'Roma', too, like 'Super Italian Paste' and 'San Marzano' (both large-fruited). But don't be without a couple of plants each of reliable hybrids like 'Beefmaster', 'Better Boy', and 'Roma'. If your season is relatively cool and short, there is good news: breeding in tomatoes (and peppers) has recently emphasized good harvests in shorter seasons. 'Stupice' is very productive for me, for instance.

You will see noted that some varieties are "determinate," others "indeterminate." All this indicates is that some (the determinates) are smaller plants, because they reach a certain size and stop growing. Indeterminate tomatoes ambitiously continue to sprout new branches until frost cuts them down.

If you are shopping for seedlings of tomatoes (or peppers and eggplants, too), don't buy ones that are in flower. Don't waste money on giant transplants; 3 to 6 inches high is perfect, so long as the seedling is

ing generous and have some left over from the roses, I give them a dose, too. (Buy it in half-gallon milk-carton-type containers at the pharmacy.)

Staked or trellised tomatoes take up less space than caged ones, but they require regular tying up and pruning of excess foliage. I cage mine in a collection of homemade wire cages, the best of which I made from concrete reinforcing wire of a large, rectangular gauge. The cages should be 18 to 24 inches across, and even at that size the biggest growers will push out quickly anyhow. For a speedy start, wrap the cages temporarily with clear heavy plastic (clamp it at the top and bottom with heavy clothespins or metal clamps from the hardware store).

If you have already purchased the pitifully undersized tomato cages from the garden center, don't despair. They work perfectly on pepper plants, which can also be staked or be supported with a peony ring. When staking is the choice with any plant, from dahlias to young trees to vegetables, insert the stake at planting time to avoid accidentally damaging the root system later.

Surprisingly, peppers prefer the deep planting method, too—right up close to the topmost set of leaves. Both peppers and eggplants also like a bit of sulfur, one folksy old gardening tradition states, and the way to give it to them is to tear the covers off a few books of paper matches and place some matches in each hole when planting. Don't fertilize peppers before they set fruit, because too much nitrogen early on gives lots of green growth but little in the way of flowers or peppers. Good soil should suffice. Eggplants can get by on a light side-dressing of fertilizer once a month. An eggplant hint: Snip off all but about five blossoms per plant for bigger fruits.

Flea beetles—which chew tiny holes in the leaves —stopped me from trying eggplants after a few bad years. Then I learned that later planting can help,

stocky and full; the plant will quickly catch up. Even after it's safely in the ground and growing, pick off the first flowers that form, to allow the plant to attain some size first.

Tomatoes will produce best if they are well rooted, so bury them deep, right down to the topmost pair or two of leaves. They are able to root all along their stems if you plant them sideways, in a trench (or extra-deep in the conventional manner). Dig a small trench about 6 to 8 inches deep and almost as long as the plant (including its root ball) is tall. Lay the plant horizontally in the trench, gently bending the top end upward, and bury all but that end and its upper pair or two of leaves.

Because my soil is acidic, I give tomatoes a dose of lime in the planting hole, along with bonemeal and an organic fertilizer labeled for vegetables. They also seem to benefit from a dose of Epsom salts (a few tablespoons to $\frac{1}{4}$ cup per plant), so if I am feel-

Tomato cages ready for duty as plants grow.

after flea beetles pass their prime. A floating row cover of Reemay fabric, forming a barrier to many insects but allowing light and moisture through, may also help, but it will have to be removed for pollination. A friend who is an organic gardener swears by a dust he makes from diatomaceous earth, fireplace ashes, and a little rotenone (an insecticide made from pyrethrum flowers), which he also uses against bean and potato beetles.

If frost is predicted, drape Reemay or an old tarp or blanket over the tomatoes; unless the weather pattern lasts for days, the overnight protection will probably spare them. If I have a lot of green tomatoes in late summer and a chill is in the air, I prune the the topmost leader back to the main plant and remove any new side shoots, to tell the plant to stop growing and start ripening. Or else I get out my recipe for mock mincemeat and chop up the green tomatoes with apples, sugar, some raisins, onions, garlic, and spices, and then can it for a holiday pie.

SALAD

Even in a cold climate, growing salad greens can be a nearly year-round accomplishment, if you have a cold frame of some sort (an outdoor shelter, usually a box with a clear lid) and also purchase a range of appropriate varieties of seeds for each season.

Unfortunately, many gardeners enjoy only that first harvest of lettuce, in early summer from a spring planting, which then bolts (stretches up its flower stalk) and goes by in a bitter-tasting farewell.

A mere 10 lettuce seeds, sown every 10 days from late winter through late summer, the earliest ones started indoors for setout later, will guarantee a family of four plenty of fresh, succulent salad greens from early spring through late fall. Don't plant 10 feet of row lettuce at a time—3 to 4 feet at most is more like it, since lettuce doesn't keep. And even with those 10 seeds, I like to mix it up a bit, alternating 5 each of two varieties at each planting, so I have a blend of colors, tastes, and textures in every bowlful.

There are three basic categories of lettuces, the earliest being the looseleaf kind, which take only 45 to 60 days to mature. 'Black-Seeded Simpson', at 45 days, is about the quickest, so don't be without it. Another nonheading lettuce I always grow is 'Oakleaf', which has beautiful ruffled leaves shaped like its namesake's. There is a red form, too, which is a nice contrast. Looseleaf lettuces are the best candidates for cut-and-come-again harvesting, yielding up to four harvests from a planting, or you can wait until maturity and pull the entire head. When the leaves reach 4 to 6 inches, simply cut them off with a sharp knife or scissors, then water well and feed the planting with a dose of fish emulsion and seaweed solution to help it regrow.

The butterhead or Bibb lettuces mature next, at 60 to 75 days, and though they do form heads, they are not so firm as the latest category, at 75-plus days, which comprises the romaines and the crispheads (including the notorious supermarket star, 'Iceberg'). The original 'Bibb' lettuce, an old-fashioned lettuce also listed as 'Limestone' on restaurant menus, has the typical buttery texture of the former group, but 'Buttercrunch' is a more modern butterhead, with a bit more texture. There are red Bibbs, too, a welcome development.

The red trend in salad "greens" continues right

A mere 10 lettuce seeds, sown every 10 days from late winter through late summer, the earliest ones started indoors for setout later, will guarantee a family of four plenty of fresh, succulent salad greens from early spring through late fall.

through the last category, the slowpoke crispheads and romaines. I have grown 'Rouge d'Hiver', a red romaine, and 'Rosy', which was the first really red crisphead type.

Lettuce seeds should never be covered too deeply; press them into a shallow furrow created with a cultivator's tines (or the point of a pencil), about ¼ inch deep. Mist, rather than blast, the area regularly so it stays moist—lettuces love moisture and will reward you by growing fast and tender. Gardeners who have been frustrated by germination failure in the hot, dry days of summer may wish to keep right on sowing their lettuce indoors every 10 days instead, then moving transplants outside as they mature. Give them a bit of shade in midsummer by planting on the cooler side of a tomato or inside the legs of the bean tepee, where it stays shadier and moister than in the open. Another germination trick is to sow in the garden, mist the bed, then place a board or a piece of burlap over the row to keep it cool and moist until the seeds begin to germinate.

Spacing of lettuce depends not only on the type but also on the harvesting method. The cut-and-come-again approach means more plants per square foot (like four); to let a crisphead mature in place, give it almost a foot to itself. I like to let my lettuces grow to medium size and then pull the head, roots and all, because they store so well with their roots dangling in a glass of water indoors on the kitchen counter, or in a bowl half-filled with water in the fridge. If I want a blend of many tastes and colors, I pick the outer leaves from this and that and use them right away, since cut leaves never last as long as whole heads.

Beyond true lettuces, the salad bowl can be filled at odd times of the year or supplemented in the main season with superhardy alternatives such as mâche, also known as corn salad, a very small plant that makes ground-hugging rosettes of leaves that are mild-tasting and soft-textured. Mâche is so cold-resistant that it sometimes grows all winter, during

thaws, and I have sown it in fall and picked it during warmish spells right through the following spring.

Spinach also makes a good addition to salads, and because it likes cool weather and bolts in summer heat, I sow it in the fall, too, or in late winter during a thaw; the seeds will germinate as soon as conditions permit, and the first pickings will come a month or so earlier than those from seeds sown when the ground can be worked in spring, about St. Patrick's Day. Beet greens are likewise good, particularly very red ones like 'Bull's Blood' and 'MacGregor's Favorite'. Pick them young. Arugula is another must, and it will gladly self-sow, as will most salad crops, if allowed to flower and set seed at the previous season's end. I usually find a dozen or more tiny plants strewn around the garden and leave them to grow, since they will beat even my earliest

An uprooted head of lettuce, like an edible summer-time bouquet.

sowing. Finally, I plant plainleaf parsley, the 'Giant Italian' kind, which is technically biennial, although I replant it every year, and sorrel (*Rumex acetosa*), a perennial salad ingredient with lemony-sour leaves.

Even heat-tolerant lettuces appreciate a bit of shade, which in the jungle of the midsummer garden is easier to find than a spot of sun at ground level. I plant lettuce seedlings inside pole-bean tepees, for example, and on the shadier side of tomatoes. Remember, anywhere there's an open square foot, three or four more heads in progress can coexist.

Don't hesitate to try a dozen different lettuces a season; a seed packet of each is too much for one season, but the seeds will remain viable for as long as six years if kept cool and dry. Since lettuce seeds are small and relatively difficult to sow thinly, I have recently started to use pelletized seed—seeds coated with a harmless material so they look like small beads of candy you'd use to decorate a cake and are easy to handle individually. Johnny's Selected Seeds has them, as do other seed houses such as Stokes (see Sources), both for lettuces and for other difficult seeds, including carrots—perhaps the most challenging of all to sow.

Inevitably, with all those lettuce varieties, there will be a small number of seeds left in some packets, and rather than save a few of this and a half-dozen of that separately, I tap them into a small recycled mayonnaise jar along with "extra" arugula, other lettuces, beet greens, and spinach and thus over the course of a season accumulate the stock of my own mesclun—a mix of salad greens—for next spring. You can buy premixed seeds blended for spicy mescluns or colorful ones, but I like to make my own. I broadcast these in early spring in a large block in the garden (maybe 2 feet by 2 feet) and pluck or shear (with scissors) whatever leaves of the mix look good at a given time for a spontaneous, everchanging salad blend.

LATE-START VEGETABLE GARDEN

Sometimes spring is cruel. It rains (or snows) every weekend, and then a late frost knocks flat the seedlings you did manage to squeeze in. Chipmunks eat the peas before they germinate (not once, but two or three replantings), and then a baby woodchuck crawls under the fence and has at the salad.

I believe in being flexible, a faith the weather has instilled in me. If it is too late for spinach, I grow chard. The Japanese green called mizuna won't mind a late start either, and in fact neither will a lot of other crops. Even well into mid- or late June, squash and beans can still find their place in the garden.

In years when spring has been a total disaster, whether owing to bad weather or to some other activity that kept me from my chores outdoors, I have resorted to Jack-in-the-Beanstalk kinds of plants that actually like it hot. Cucumbers will quickly cover the trellis where the springtime peas failed; summer and winter squash, gourds, and pumpkins will gladly camouflage all evidence of your late start to the season, and then some. So will extra-showy and also edible pole beans like 'Scarlet Runner'. Zinnias, cosmos, nasturtiums, signet marigolds ('Lemon Gem' and 'Tangerine Gem'), and the smaller, multiflowered branching sunflowers do just fine started anytime in June in my area, a month or more after the optimum moment. The message: Don't give up if you get off to a late start, just refigure your plans with heat lovers and fast growers.

When all else fails, announce to anyone who casts a critical eye at your vegetable garden that you left it sparse this year on purpose, because you plan to buy bargain-priced "liners" of perennials—young perennials in cell-packs about the way that tomato seedlings come—and grow them on for planting out in fall or the following spring. Or say you plan to start your own flowers from seed and transplant

LEFT **Raised beds have some early salad sprouting.**
RIGHT **Raised beds in summer, with beans ascending a tepee made of three poles.**

them into the vegetable garden to grow on a couple of seasons—the cheapest way of all to have perennials and biennials for the flower garden, provided you can wait. Or explain that it is an organic approach to bug control, since earlier plantings of beans, cucumbers, and squash, in particular, are susceptible to beetles (beans and cucumbers) and borers (squash and cucumbers) that summer sowings typically escape some of the impact of. A May sowing of beans might yield three pickings; a July one, up to five. A friend and I call this the Never-Too-Late Theory, and because of it we are always right on time with our gardening plans.

PLANT SUPPORTS

Perhaps because I have always had poor posture, I do not take naturally to staking. I find it hard to make my plants stand up straight, too, although practice is having its good effect. But early training, when plants are still youthful and supple, will result in a much more natural-looking and effective means of support than a stake driven in beside a hollyhock that is already burgeoning under its own weight with a thunderstorm brewing in the sky.

Different strategies suit different plants, and other peoples' gardens—public and private—often yield as many clever techniques for support as they do new planting ideas. The feats of engineering are especially impressive if they either disappear under the growth of the plant, doing their job quietly but effectively, or stand out as an ornamental feature in their own right while performing the support role.

Some kinds of supports should be used only in the former way, like peony rings or so-called grow-throughs, metal grids on legs that the plant grows up and through. There is nothing attractive about these; they're just good tools. Install them when the plants are perhaps a foot out of the ground, and let the plants grow up into the supports while camouflaging them. Peony rings are effective with plants other than peonies, too, like the shrubby, nonvining clema-

tis (*Clematis recta,* for instance). They can also be adapted by inserting sticks of brush inside, like the vertical bones of a corset, to further truss up the plants within. Stakes, whether metal or bamboo, add little to the look of a garden but can detract if they're placed badly. Get them in early, whether for a tomato or a dahlia or some other creature, and continue tying the plant up as it grows so the stake stays hidden inside the expanding growth.

Sometimes stakes, particularly natural bamboo or rustic ones culled from tree prunings, can be rigged together so they rate being seen, at least a bit. For instance, a railing fashioned of bamboo canes lashed together with twine could hold up a bed of medium- to large-size plants, such as ornamental grasses, that might otherwise flop into a path.

Tripods or tepees made of bamboo or branches are actually attractive enough to serve as a focal point, even in winter when no plant is growing on them. Three or four poles or branches set into the ground and then tied together at the top, in the shape of a tepee, make a great support for annual vines, beans, shorter clematis, and even some roses, if the tripod is large enough. To help less sturdy vines get started up the tepee, try attaching a panel of netting (the lightweight black polypropylene kind) around the lower half of the support.

Whatever the plant, I leave the metal hoops up over the winter rather than carry them in and out each year. Sometimes I am lucky and tepees last more than a year—it all depends on the wood I salvaged from the winter's cleanup, how thick it was, and whether it had natural rot resistance.

Plants that always seem to split open in the middle, like perennial baby's breath (*Gypsophila paniculata*) or even a hydrangea like white-flowered *Hydrangea arborescens* 'Annabelle', can be corseted with a set of bamboo stakes driven in around the base. Garden twine should be laced around each stake and all the way around the plant at a couple of heights as the plant grows, until it has sufficient sup-

Different strategies suit different plants, and other peoples' gardens—public and private—
often yield as many clever techniques for support as they do new planting ideas.

port. The stakes and should be low enough to be hidden when the plant arches up and over the corset—the right effect, since these plants aren't meant to be stiff, upright cylinders staked up high.

To pick an appropriate method of support is first to conjure the image of the plant in your mind's eye. Match plant to tactic so the effect is natural.

Brush collected from spring cleanup or pruning can also be called into action as a plant support, limited only by your creative engineering abilities and the shapes and sizes of materials available. Brush with one strong, straight end that fans out and forks into several branches at the other end is good because many pieces can be "planted," straight end down, all the way around a floppy plant. They will form a rustic, romantic enclosure that will never look like a sore thumb, the way store-bought things can. I use a dibble—that T-shaped, pointed tool that's good for planting large seeds or small bulbs—to make holes in the ground in which to insert the branch ends, then backfill and tamp well to make certain they are secure. Laced with twine, brush supports will be even stronger.

Although most things that need staking should get attention early, there are exceptions. Really late bloomers, such as asters, *Salvia leucantha,* and sneezeweed (*Helenium autumnale*), should be propped only when they need it, usually well into their growing season. The sneezeweed, for instance, has perfectly stout stems, but when its many flowers form it gets itself into trouble. It needs your help just before that critical moment.

And there's one more option: eliminating the need to stake altogether. Many late-blooming perennials—including larger asters and heleniums, and Montauk daisy (*Chrysanthemum nipponicum*)—can be cut back once or even several times from mid-spring to early summer, so they get bushier and fuller and don't topple. But beware: If you cut back a

The vegetable garden in summer, with tithonia, cosmos, and other cutting flowers in full force, too.

springtime bloomer in spring, it may fail to flower until the following year.

CUTTING-GARDEN SCHEME

There are tulips in the vegetable garden, poking up from between the rhubarb leaves, and at the ends of each raised bed there are a dozen more—each group a different kind.

This is the way I grow a cutting garden without having to work another area of the yard—without extra weeding, or mulching, or tilling. When the vegetable garden winds down in fall and it is bulb-planting time, I tuck tulips in every spot not destined for early-spring vegetables—the spots that remain vacant until Memorial Day, such as the areas for tomatoes, peppers, eggplants, and basil. I will cut the tulips and use them indoors as they flower, for about six weeks in April and May. Then I pull the bulbs, since they seldom return reliably. (Using so-called perennializing tulips would be an alternative to my method, and they last for several years.)

I also leave a bit of room at the ends of my long raised vegetable beds for flowers, to dress the garden up a bit. In spring I grow calendula (from seeds) and pansies and then stocks (from nursery seedlings); tithonia and zinnias go in as summer unfolds. A dozen or two gladiolus corms planted every week from May through July yield regular vasefuls (I especially love the violet and chartreuse ones

and recommend planting varieties with shorter stems, not 5-footers). They find a place along the edge of beds or behind a row of salad crops, beside a fence. Leave room for at least a dahlia plant or two for late cut flowers.

Because one purpose is to make my vegetable garden more beautiful than it would be with food crops alone, I pick a color scheme, which makes the vegetable garden look more designed. Whatever the main color—orange and purple are two great choices that go well with vegetables such as tomatoes—I always make room for lots of chartreuse flowers, since chartreuse works well with any flower-arranging scheme. 'Envy' zinnias, 'Lime Green' nicotiana, and the smaller-flowered *Nicotiana langsdorffii*, for example, are musts.

Training roses up an archway over your vegetable-garden gate is another way to put cutting flowers into your food-garden scheme, without sacrificing major food-growing space. Just be careful not to cast too much shade with the ornamentals—particularly those on the south and western borders of the plot—since few vegetables will tolerate it.

EVERYTHING'S AN ANNUAL

By botanical definition, an annual is a plant that goes through its life cycle, from germination to setting its own crop of seed and dying, in a single growing year. But to a gardener an annual should be more than just those typical bedding plants that follow that precise biological clock. An annual should simply be defined as any plant that you don't count on to overwinter outdoors but are happy to enjoy outside in the warm months—a temporary but nevertheless cherished feature of the warm-season garden.

By that definition, the marigolds you buy in flats at the garden center are still annuals. And so are most of what we grow as vegetables. But this reinterpretation of the term means that anything from a red-variegated banana tree to some of the Mexican ornamental salvias, to houseplants like small-leaved ivies and showy-leaved begonias, can be used as annuals, too.

In a slide lecture once, a city gardener showed a bedding scheme he'd done that was edged in snake plant (*Sansevieria*), one of the toughest "houseplants" of all. Apparently there had been a real bargain on them at the Woolworth's houseplant department that summer, and he'd thought "Why not?" and scooped up several dozen. They looked like a living green picket fence—very architectural, and unlike virtually any of the more expected plants he might have chosen. At season's end he had the choice of either digging them up to take indoors or throwing them away. (A lot of neighbors landed free houseplants that fall.)

Many worthwhile bulbs and bulblike plants are not hardy in cold-winter zones like mine, but I can set them out in spring and grow them as annuals, too, then either lift and store them or buy new ones for the following year. *Crocosmia, Acidanthera, Gladiolus, Canna, Calla, Dahlia, Colocasia* (elephant's ear), and *Caladium* are some possibilities.

The vegetable world can yield many fine ornamental annuals to be used elsewhere in the yard, such as 'Ruby' chard, with its brilliant red midribs; the red-stemmed variety of climbing Malabar spinach; 'Scarlet Runner' beans; and even frilly pars-

ABOVE **Tubers of elephant's ears on the kitchen counter (with other gleanings from the landscape) before planting.** BELOW **Elephant's ears in their first summer; they must be lifted and stored for winter.**

ley. Dill and the similarly ferny 'Bronze Fennel', which has a smoky wine cast, rate a place in certain flower-garden designs, too. Even some of the prettiest red-leaved lettuces would be beautiful as edging.

Don't slander plants by labeling them as one thing or another. Whether they are technically perennials or biennials or whatever, tropical or subtropical or temperate in origin, if they appeal to you visually, see if you can find a place to enjoy them in your garden, if only for a few months each year.

VIBURNUMS

It was the stately double-file viburnum (*Viburnum plicatum tomentosum*) that got me started in this outstanding genus of flowering and fruiting shrubs. The double-file is a plant whose habit of growth is so distinctive that I could not help but notice it. It stands with its branches held straight outward, like so many arms outstretched, and in spring they are completely covered with white flowers.

Today I either possess or covet many of its cousins, like the highly aromatic *V. carlesii*, the Korean spice viburnum, with daphnelike fragrance from barely pink-flushed white flowers in late April. You can smell it across the yard even when it is young; by the time this rounded plant reaches maturity, you will smell it down the road. *V.* × *juddii*, Judd's viburnum, is also highly perfumed (*V. carlesii* is one of its parents), as is *V.* × *burkwoodii*.

In soggy spots try the European cranberry bush, *V. opulus,* which produces maple-shaped leaves that have a reddish fall cast and red fall fruit. Its native counterpart is *V. trilobum,* another informal shrub with bright fruit.

V. 'Watanabe' blooms off and on all season, May through summer's end—how many other shrubs promise that? It is a compact version of the double-file, reaching only 6 feet or so, an outstanding choice for yards that can't take the small-tree size of the double-file. If you can accommodate a larger scale, the varieties 'Mariesii' and 'Shasta' are recom-

The cranberry bush *Viburnum* in flower.

mended. The double-file viburnum has another feature: handsome fall color, from a burnished wine color to smoky purple—another reason to include one in the landscape.

I also grow a couple of rangy plants of a leather-leaf viburnum, *V. rhytidophyllum*—the only shrub that actually doesn't seem to care when the deer totally defoliate it every winter and even disfigure its shape. The foliage, as the name suggests, is basically evergreen, and the plants seem to bloom off and on through the summer and fall. There are better forms, with leaves less coarse than those of my specimens, including *V.* × *pragense*.

The only complaint I have with the viburnums is that the fruit I had read about, and hoped to enjoy in the fall garden, almost never lasts long enough to even ripen fully. Viburnums are like giant bird feeders, and no matter how big they are, they can be picked clean in a flash. I am told that a couple of species fare better against the hungry creatures, including *V. dilatatum* 'Erie' or just plain *V. dilatatum*. The tea viburnum, *V. setigerum,* is tall and leggy, and when its branches are laden with fruit they actually bend toward the ground. With that much of a crop, perhaps there will be enough for my visual feast in fall and the birds' gustatory one.

SHRUBS FROM CUTTINGS

There's always some plant you'd like more of—whether for your own garden or to share with admiring visitors. Many shrubs and some vines can be propagated in early summer from softwood cuttings —wood that by about mid-June or so onward in my garden, but before late summer into fall, when it hardens off, is soft but not too soft. (If you can cut a piece of the shrub one morning and put it in a glass of water overnight, and it doesn't wilt, the wood is just right for propagating.) Boston ivy, honeysuckle, trumpet vine, wisteria, and even some clematis are possible candidates, as are weigela, cotoneaster, spirea, buddleia, roses, privet, willow, and many others.

In the morning, when the plants are at their maximum moisture level, gather cuttings from the parent plant in an out-of-the-way spot. Although you need cuttings with only about three pairs of leaves (more in plants whose leaves are tightly spaced along the stems), make longer cuttings to trim later indoors. Make extras, because there will be losses.

You will need a flat of rooting medium such as moistened vermiculite, perlite, or a blend, whether divided into individual cells or not. A plastic cover (or one rigged of dry-cleaning bags and coat hangers) will keep the cuttings moist once they are planted.

Working on a table, trim the cuttings down by removing the topmost pair of leaves, which would wilt anyhow. Trim the stem immediately below the lowest pair you want to save, just below what is called the leaf node (usually a little bump on the stem from which the leaves emerge). Then remove those bottom leaves, and any fruit or flowers, and dip the end of the cutting first into clear water and then into a saucer into which you have poured a little bit of rooting hormone powder (don't dip into the can and don't put what's left in the saucer back in).

Use a pencil to poke a hole in the center of each cell of the planting medium, so that the powder will stay on the cutting when you insert it. After you put the cutting in the hole, firm well around it so the contact between the medium and the stem is really solid, using a chopstick or your finger. Label every kind of cutting, and cover with a plastic tent or domed lid. Place the flat in bright light, artificial or natural, but not direct sun.

Cuttings take from several weeks to two months to root; a gentle tug after a few weeks, if met with resistance, indicates that roots have begun to take hold. Check regularly to see if misting is needed, and remove any cuttings that wilt or begin to decay. Once the cuttings are rooted, feed them with soluble fertilizer mixed at half-strength every two weeks, and when they have a presentable network of roots to rely on, slowly wean them from the moist tent and then pot them up individually in potting soil. Care for them outdoors in a protected spot, and then in late fall, when they go dormant, either pack them into a cold frame with mulch around the pots or plunge them into the soil, pots and all, then mulch around the buried pots. They need a winter outdoors.

Depending on the growth rate of each type of plant, they may be big enough for a place of their own in the garden the following year or not until as much as a couple of years later, in which case they may need repotting or placement in a nursery area.

OPPOSITE **The double-file viburnum in bloom.**
BELOW **Weigela can be started from cuttings.**

PLANTING IN THE CRACKS

The most satisfying garden-making experience I have had so far wasn't meant to be a garden at all. It was meant to be a walkway, formed of fieldstones fit like a loose puzzle into a series of irregular steps from the driveway to the front door. What had once been a hard-to-navigate, uneven area of grass was intended to be more conducive to safe transit from there to here.

It didn't exactly turn out that way, however.

The sandy cracks and crevices in the walkway were just too tempting. Before I'd even used the new steps for a week, I was out buying crack-and-crevice plants to tuck in here and there—low-growing sedums, woolly yarrow (*Achillea tomentosa*), *Ajuga,* creeping thymes, and the like. Before a month had passed, I didn't want anybody to walk on the path at all.

Today the path is what I call my front garden, and it is shown in photograph after photograph in this book as an example of how even a small area like a walkway can become a four-season garden, with something to look at most of the year.

Except for the fact that I still have to walk across the lawn to get to the front door, the walkway has been a great success. With this happy experience in mind, I have since installed a large patio on one side of the house, and as you might guess it isn't meant to be furnished or otherwise used as a patio at all. It's a crack-and-crevice garden, or a paved garden, as these are sometimes called, and it is in the process of coming of age.

1 Both the walkway and the patio are set without mortar, on a base of builder's sand. There is a firm bed of soil beneath the top 4 to 6 inches of sand, of course, but when I go to transplant a thyme or sow a seed in either of my paved gardens, the medium in which I'm working between the cracks is basically pure sand. Somewhat surprisingly to me, a wide diversity of plants seem just fine with this medium, even though sand is completely inorganic (that is, it's not composed of formerly living materials like humus that help hold moisture and nutrients). It's also fast-draining almost to a fault. But the fact that the plants can bask in the warmth of the paving stones —like so many solar collectors— while simultaneously having their roots tucked under a cool, moist place seems to delight them.

Planting in tight spaces requires some special tools, among them a bamboo cane cut down to about a foot long, a small trowel or sturdy table-spoon, a sharp knife (a grafting knife or kitchen knife), a butter knife or other blunt-edged blade, a dibble, a whisk broom, and a small bucket or large flowerpot.

2 First I space my plants out where I intend to place them. Generally speaking, for this purpose large plants are not worth the cost. Young transplants are better, since they root in fast and don't suffer so much shock.

3 Even with medium-size plants of creeping thyme, I may use a sharp kitchen knife or a grafting knife to divide the root balls into a couple of wedges, because many cracks are too tight for anything more.

4 I excavate the sand from the pocket I plan to plant, using the small trowel, and reserve it some-where in the bucket or flowerpot for when a stone sinks a bit and needs reseating after winter. Then I tease apart the root ball of the transplant a bit, tuck it in, and backfill with some of the sand.

5 Using the short bamboo cane, I tamp the sand around the plant to get it securely in the pocket, eliminating any air spaces below.

6 When a whole area is planted, I first brush off the stone a bit, then use a sprinkler to slowly water the area over the course of at least half an hour.

Everything will try to gain a foothold in your paved garden, since the warmth and sandy medium are magnets for self-sowns, including weeds, and here's where the butter knife comes in. Make a weekly patrol

and use the blunt knife to dig out any unwanted plants before they root in under the stones.

As for how much foot traffic crack plants can take, it varies. Besides lawn grass, which I keep out of my paved gardens, moss can take about the most, and then comes creeping thyme. Succulents, like sedum and portulaca, or even the yellow-flowered *Corydalis lutea,* don't bounce back well because their fleshy parts get crushed or broken off. It doesn't kill them, but they look a wreck. Snow-in-summer (*Cerastium*) is another good crack plant, and fairly durable, but, like woolly yarrow, doesn't want to be mashed into the ground either. I also like to use some unconventional choices in the cracks, such as an occasional *Geranium renardii* or *Heuchera* or even an ornamental salvia, and a mound of wormwood, and they do not want to be stepped on at all. Try to leave a pathway through, planted only in durable, prostrate thymes or not at all.

The same basic ideas work when you have a stone wall and want to make it a garden. The plants are a little harder to get going in a vertical space, since they (and the soil around them) are inclined to wash or fall out. A strip of turfgrass (cut from your lawn, soil and all) can be used as a nurse medium to start a young plant going in a large pocket in a wall. Pretend it is a jelly roll: the transplant is the filling and the turf is the cake. Roll the transplant's root system up inside the turf, soak the whole roll, then stuff it into the wall pocket. Water the turf roll regularly with a mister until the plant gets established.

Seeds are best blown into cracks, rather than planted by hand. First moisten the soil in the pocket with a mist bottle, then place the seeds in the V of an index card folded lengthwise. Move the seed-filled card up to the crack, and blow them in with your breath. A small piece of tissue or toilet paper can be placed over the seeds and misted again, to act as a biodegradable mulch until they germinate.

MARCH

THE FRONT WALK THROUGH THE SEASONS

SEPTEMBER

JUNE

DECEMBER

ALLIUMS

I first grew alliums in self-defense: the chipmunks, squirrels, rabbits, woodchucks, and deer had had too good a time devouring my crocus, tulips, and lilies, and so I was determined to plant things they wouldn't eat. Besides *Narcissus*, which are poisonous, the next most unappealing bulb genus is *Allium*.

I began with the usual suspects: the June-blooming kinds with large purple globes atop long stems, ones like *A. giganteum* and *A. aflatunense*. There are others of this classic allium appearance: *A. rosenbachianum* (a bit earlier and shorter than *A. giganteum*); and 'Globemaster', with giant heads.

But *Allium* is much more than purple spheres. For the look of fireworks exploding, there is the star-tling *A. schubertii*, about 2 feet high with a foot or wider lilac-pink loose sphere on top. There is tiny *A. moly*, which carries its bright yellow flowers on 8-inch stems. I have it in the cracks in my fieldstone patio, where it seems perfectly happy, and I expect it would be as easy in a conventional garden bed. *A. christophii* is a real winner, with nearly foot-wide heads of a silvery lavender that are airy, not dense. I plant it in a mass of lady's mantle (*Alchemilla mollis*), since it coincides in bloom time and seems to hover just above the *Alchemilla*'s chartreuse sprays. It is exceptionally long-lasting, looking good for many weeks while blooming and then for many weeks more while turning a straw color. I like the faded look

right in the garden, but I eventually carry off some for indoor use, where they last literally for years.

There is rose-pink *A. unifolium;* a number of species, including *A. rosenbachianum,* come in white forms; *A. caeruleum* is a true blue; and don't forget the most familiar alliums of all, common chives (*A. schoenoprasum,* with lilac springtime blooms) and garlic chives (*A. neapolitanum,* which bears white flowers in summer). There is even one to grow for its foliage alone, *A. karativiense,* which has large, low, blue foliage topped with pale mauve puffs. All the bulbous ones are planted in fall, in a sunny spot where the soil drains well.

PERENNIAL GERANIUMS

I was many years into gardening before I knew that a geranium (that tender plant with coral-red flowers that people pot up in window boxes and planters by the millions each year) was no *Geranium* at all. Like the misnamed "scented geraniums," it's actually in the genus *Pelargonium*. The true *Geranium* is a com-pletely different plant. My first encounter was with the accommodating and beautiful *G. macrorrhizum,* or bigroot geranium. I saw it growing as a flowering ground cover for shade in a public garden in New York City and was taken by its attractive leaves, which the gardener told me were nearly evergreen and even took on a reddish cast in the cooler weather.

ABOVE, LEFT TO RIGHT **Allium karativiense; a mix of alliums; 'Globemaster' and *A. rosenbachianum* 'Album'; *christophii*.** OPPOSITE **The classic globular allium flower.**

A bonus: The bigroot geranium, if touched, emits an aromatic, spicy scent, the way that artemisias and bee balms do—a kind of smell I like as much as the sweeter perfumes of lilies and roses. This species is actually adaptable to sun or shade and is available in forms with white, dark pink, or paler pink flowers. The blooms come in early June, and when they fade a few weeks later, I simply cut them off to enjoy the hummocky mound of the plant, through which no weeds penetrate.

There are other geraniums for shade, including *G. phaeum,* which has large leaves and tiny, very dark purple or white flowers. *G. p.* 'Samobor' has leaves marked in bands of the darkest red-purple, and there is a variegated cultivar, *G. p.* 'Variegatus', to covet. Although the phaeum flowers are small, you will still cherish them.

Among the other geranium standouts for sunnier spots are the golden-leaved hybrid 'Ann Folkard', which offers wonderfully raucous, magenta-purple flowers as a counterpoint to its leaves; and 'Birch Double', also called 'Plenum', a form of *G. himalayense* with nicely cut leaves over which hover violet puffy flowers. One of the most popular is 'Johnson's Blue', a hybrid with a long show of lavender-blue flowers and attractive, divided foliage.

There are tiny members of the genus and giants, in both leaf size and overall scale of the plants; ones that mound neatly and others that sprawl and clamber. Almost across the board, I find their foliage at least as interesting as their flowers. The geraniums are easy to grow, and many among them make fine ground covers or even underplantings to shrubs such as roses, which they complement nicely. As fillers to the flower garden, they are some of the best plants going, holding their space attractively even when not in bloom.

FUMITORIES

I am intrigued by the relationships between plants, and it has become something of a theme for my purchases. I find one thing I like and then want to know what it's related to, and try that, and so on. Lately, I am taken with what are called fumitories—the bleeding heart (*Dicentra*) and its cousins in the genera *Corydalis* and *Adlumia*. Taxonomically, they are close relatives of the poppy family.

The name *fumitory* derives from the Latin words meaning "smoke of the earth," and their foliage does have a grayish blue or yellowish bronze cast, like smoke, in some cases. It also looks like it might melt in your hand, like a puff of smoke. Quite to the contrary, these are easy, reliable plants that will stay around just about forever.

My garden came with little in the way of assets: a couple of ancient lilacs, a somewhat dubiously valuable evergreen rhododendron about 15 feet high and wide, and several giant clumps of bleeding heart, *Dicentra spectabilis,* with its bright pink flowers. This exceptionally easy plant should be in every garden. I like to cut its arching flower stalks for springtime arrangements, and every year I find myself in renewed disbelief that such an intricate, cunning flower form could possibly have evolved. The pure white form called 'Alba' is smaller and less vigorous.

The only drawback, particularly in hotter zones (or unusually hot summers in cooler zones), is that the common bleeding heart goes dormant. For me, this may be as late as mid-August, mostly because my big, old plants are shaded and in good, moist soil. Its exit is a prelude of fall, since it slowly turns a

ABOVE **The nearly evergreen leaves of *Geranium macrorrhizum.*** BELOW **A big clump of bleeding heart; its delicate vining cousin, *Adlumia fungosa.***

delightful honey color as it goes to sleep. But if it happens in July, one must be ready with some backup—a large potted plant, or a quick-covering annual already in place and starting to take off, such as elephant's ear (*Colocasia*)—because the gap can be as big as 3 feet across.

A number of its close cousins, though not quite as large or spectacular, keep at it all season, blooming from May through frost. Probably the best known is *D. eximia,* the fringed bleeding heart, which bears smaller magenta or pink flowers on 1- to 1½-foot-tall plants with very ferny foliage. It is inclined to sow itself around the flower garden in an inoffensive manner. There is also a white variety, *D. e.* 'Alba', with the same agreeable traits. *D. eximia* is a native American, hailing from the East. Its western counterpart, *D. formosa,* is quite similar, but friends in the Northwest tell me its self-sowing can make it a pest.

The first *Corydalis* I ever grew was the ultra-easy *C. flexuosa,* which produces yellow flowers from midspring through fall and beautiful, ferny foliage. It sows itself around but is easy to pull out. Lately, the astonishing-looking electric-blue-flowered *Corydalis* are the rage, such as *C. f.* 'Blue Panda', and there are purple-blue forms now, too. A climbing *Dicentra, D. scandens,* offering delicate foliage and yellow flowers, is suddenly popular. Old-fashioned *Adlumia fungosa,* a climbing cousin that is a native American, behaves as a biennial for me and also self-sows around. It has pinkish white flowers and is very ambitious.

EUPHORBIAS

Probably the most familiar *Euphorbia* of all is the poinsettia, *E. pulcherrima,* but it is many zones too tender and also many shades too vulgar for my home garden. In dismissing it, however, I do not wish to imply that I am not a fan of euphorbias, also known as spurges, because if there is one genus I wish had more hardy members, this is it. Euphorbias are colorful over a very long period, especially when compared with many other plants.

Euphorbia polychroma with blue spikes of **Ajuga** fill the cracks in the front walk in spring.

Unfortunately, in Zone 5, I have to rely on the toughest of the lot. One of the most reliably cheery plants of early spring is the familiar, widely available *E. polychroma,* with its startling bracts as golden yellow as a goldfinch in summer. It seems hardy, and after starting out with only one plant years ago, I find myself with a lifetime supply. I cut them back in late winter or earliest spring so that the buds, or growing tips, are all about the same height, encouraging the plant to develop into an even mound.

E. myrsinites doesn't look anything like *E. polychroma,* but it is a real beauty, a blue-green, sculptural plant with snaky, spiky stems like a sedum. It favors heat and dryness (great for a pocket in a stone patio), unlike the others, which prefer richer, moister soil or even the filtered bright light of an open woodland.

I am trying some of the beautiful purple-leaved euphorbias, and though I probably won't ever see any of their chartreuse to acid-yellow flowers, I am content if the plant survives so I can enjoy the rest of it. *E. dulcis* 'Chameleon', with marbled purple-green foliage, is getting attention lately and is said to be hardy in my cold zone. We'll see. *E. amygdaloides* 'Purpurea' is another standout, along with the *E. griffithii* cultivars 'Fireglow' and 'Dixter', which have startling orange flower heads. If your zone is a bit warmer, and you want color to match, try them.

FERNS

"God made ferns to show what he could do with leaves," Thoreau wrote. These ancient plants, which date back several hundred million years, evolved into a moist world where there were no flowers or seeds. Instead of blooming, relying on animal pollinators, and then setting a crop of seed, they reproduce from spores, a dustlike material that contains their living germplasm. The spores gather into what are called sori, which may resemble brown dot candy orderly arranged on the undersides of the fronds or broad brushstrokes of cinnamon-colored velvet, as on the nonhardy staghorn fern.

As garden plants, ferns are basically pest- and disease-free and require neither staking nor deadheading. What more can you ask?

A fern is not a fern is not a fern, however. Each has its own character and its own place in the garden. None is more ornamental than the Japanese painted fern (*Athyrium nipponicum* 'Pictum'), with its silver-splashed fronds and chocolate midribs. The Hart's-tongue fern (*Phyllitis scolopendrium*) has tongue-shaped fronds that can be several feet in length and up to 4 inches wide. It likes a limy spot against a wall or outcrop. Goldie's fern (*Dryopteris goldiana*) is a standout, 4 to 5 feet high and several feet wide. The autumn fern (*Dryopteris erythrosora*) has pink-bronze new growth in spring and some autumn color, too. And there are even evergreens, such as the Christmas fern (*Polystichum acrostichoides*).

ABOVE **Fresh fern fronds with columbine.** BELOW **Some rhodendron flowers float on the pond surface beneath the Japanese painted fern's variegated fronds.**

Although many ferns are shade lovers, there are ferns for sunny spots, such as sensitive fern (*Onoclea sensibilis*) and the ostrich fern (*Matteuccia struthiopteris*), both of which bear their spores on separate fronds called fertile fronds, brown wands that are very ornamental in winter or in dried arrangements. The hay-scented fern (*Dennstaedtia punctilobula*) takes sun, too, and like the other two will spread to form a large colony. In fact, there are fern species native to deserts and wetlands and rock outcroppings, so no matter what your garden challenge, there is probably a fern for the job. Specialty catalogs such as those from Fancy Fronds and Foliage Gardens (see Sources) have many unusual species and forms, including so-called crested ferns —highly ornamental ones with fronds that are even lacier than the norm.

Unlike many other perennials, ferns have rather small root systems, technically called rhizomes. They should not be buried deeply. The woodland types like humusy, well-prepared soil that is loose and full of rotted leaf mold, and they also appreciate some bonemeal worked in. A light mulch, simulating the leaves that drop and decay on the forest floor in nature, will help them settle in.

PEONIES

When all seems hopeless, I think of the peonies that grew in the narrow space between the flagstone walk and the stucco-and-brick wall at the home of my youth. No matter that there was hardly room for anything in that spot, or that they'd been there probably 30 years. Every year, during the week of my birthday, they bloomed like mad.

If the peonies could put up with such tough conditions, literally between a rock and a hard place, I figure I, too, can go on.

Although they bloom in early June, peonies are best planted or moved in early September, when specialty nurseries sell clumps by mail. Despite the fact that these are really durable creatures, the gardener

A bough of one of the old lilacs on the front lawn as it starts to fade to silvery lavender.

must do a few things right to ensure that they bloom. First, don't bury the "eyes"—the pink tips or buds on the thick peony root—any deeper than 1½ to 2 inches below the soil surface (a very deep mulch can also thwart them). Plant them in the sun: at least a half-day of strong, full sun is essential; more is better. Be sparing with nitrogen-heavy fertilizer, which promotes green, not flowers. And be patient. Young plants, or ones that have recently been moved, may take a year to settle in.

If your peonies make buds that never open into flowers but turn black instead, or if the foliage is marked with dark discolorations, the plants may have botrytis, a fungal disease that is common in wet conditions. Cut off the affected parts and put them in the trash (not in the compost heap!), and be sure to clean up around the base of the plants after frost fells the foliage, where the disease spores might overwinter and spread again in spring.

If you have not tried the single-flowered peonies, which have one row of petals and a very prominent center (instead of oodles of petals and a center that is hidden by them), do. They are simpler and more elegant than their puffy relatives. Peonies, whether single or double, are classified as to bloom season—early, mid-, and late—and choosing some from each category will mean more weeks in their company.

LILACS

Except in the warmest zones, where they are basically disinclined to flower, almost every garden should include some common lilacs (*Syringa vulgaris*), an old-fashioned shrub that couldn't be easier to grow. Given a place in full sun, good drainage, adequate air circulation (to prevent powdery mildew), and proper pruning, they will produce profuse numbers of fragrant flowers. If lilacs fail to bloom, it usually means that they have been sited where the light is poor or

If the peonies could put up with such tough conditions, literally between a rock and a hard place, I figure I, too, can go on.

have been pruned sometime other than right after flowering.

The common lilac, like other spring-blooming shrubs and trees, produces its flowers on the previous year's wood, meaning the dormant flower buds are produced from late summer through fall and carried over all winter. If you prune a lilac after about July 4, you risk reducing next year's bloom. If you prune in fall or in early spring, you definitely will lose some or all of the flowers.

Once a lilac is established, regular pruning—which amounts to nothing more than cutting off bundles of flowers every year, then removing the rest as they fade as if you were gathering bouquets—will keep a plant in shape and flowering strong. You needn't cut any more than that, so long as the plant is the basic shape and size you desire; just don't leave the flowers on to dry and set seed. Regular removal of suckers—shoots jutting up from the base —is also important, unless they figure into the future shape of the plant. Dead and damaged wood should always be removed as it appears.

An aged, out-of-shape lilac can usually be rejuvenated over the course of three years if you cut one-third of its stems to the ground each summer. That will bring the flowers down to nose height and make for a bushy plant, which all the experts talk about, but sometimes I think that's missing the point. Apparently they have never lain upstairs in bed while their 100-year-old common lilac bloomed right at mattress height. An ancient lilac, with gnarled, twisted trunks, can be a real treasure, but it will need to be cleaned out regularly in the center, deadheaded religiously, and fed and limed annually, too. It will still lose trunks to storms and age, and new growth will have to be encouraged over the years to fill in. But I've never even considered making bushy, low plants out of my pair of century-old lilacs; sometimes conventional wisdom doesn't apply. Evaluate each situation individually, not just by the book.

Although the basic lilac color is probably the most typically seen, there are also blue-lavender, deep purples, pinks, palest yellows, and whites among the common lilac, and ones that bloom early in lilac season, midseason, and late. Beyond that, the common lilac is by no means the best choice anyway, particularly for small gardens. Many other worthwhile species and hybrids deserve consideration, including the bushy, 9-foot *S. patula* 'Miss Kim', whose many smallish, silvery lilac flowers come a bit late in the lilac season. Perhaps the latest lilac, which isn't a shrub at all but a small tree, is *S. reticulata*, which has creamy, large flower heads and shiny bark reminiscent of that of a cherry tree. Unfortunately, the common lilacs tend to have the corner on that lilac smell; the others pale by comparison. To me that says at least one common lilac plant is a must.

CONNECTING THE SEASONS

I feared the worst, and then came crambe. On that difficult cusp between spring and summer—when one is over and the other not really yet begun—it takes a plant like *Crambe cordifolia* to fill the gaps left by the last of spring. Crambe looks like a giant, floppy cabbage topped in a billow of baby's breath, and when in flower it can fill a sunny spot about 5 feet across and 5 feet high.

BELOW **Goatsbeard plumes drip over the hostas in a shady spot as late spring changes to early summer.** RIGHT **A leaf of lady's mantle in the rain.**

Goatsbeard (*Aruncus dioicus*) is another easy, shrub-size perennial, a native plant that resembles a giant astilbe. It likewise can form a bridge into summer, with 6-foot plumes atop a mass of ferny, 4-foot foliage that distract you from the fact that all the irises have faded, and worse. Sited in the shade, it will be quite happy.

Thank goodness for lady's mantle (*Alchemilla mollis*), whose beautiful, blue-green leaves and chartreuse flowers catch the eye now, too. And *Allium* can help to bridge the gap; what did I dare to look at at this difficult moment before I grew these plants? *Clematis recta*, about 2½ feet tall and wider, is spilling out of the top of its support into a mass of variegated ribbon grass (*Phalaris arundinacea* 'Picta'), the grass's white stripes and the clematis's matching flowers a gleaming combination that diverts the eye from where the early peonies have faded.

The recent crop of purple-leaved *Heuchera*, like 'Montrose Ruby' and 'Ruby Veil' and the most common, 'Palace Purple', can almost carry a bed on their own, or at least draw the eye away from slightly less desirable vistas. I would not be without these showy selections of the native coralbells, which are nearly evergreen (ever-purple?), even under the snow in my cold garden. Some dwarf red barberries have the similar effect: thank goodness they're not ratty or in need of deadheading (cutting off the faded blossoms) like so many other once lovely plants are looking in latest June.

The last moments of spring, or the first of summer, can be rough on a garden and a gardener—with all the chores, it's hard to see what's any good about gardening anyhow. On the other side, when summer comes on in full force with its own look, we will remember the plants that helped us over the hurdle. Such season connectors will come to be thought of as the gardener's best of friends.

CONFIDENCE BUILDERS

I think that every gardener deserves a boost in confidence when new to horticulture and therefore recommend my list of certified confidence builders as starter plants. They are a mismatched lot, with vigor their only common trait. Bee balm (*Monarda didyma*) heads the list, adapting as it will to sun or half-shade and growing about a mile—sideways—a year. It does what its name implies and draws the bees, a quality I like near my vegetable garden.

Bee balm is in the mint family; its intense aroma, square stems (a characteristic of many mint family members), and aggressive underground deportment give it away. I still grow it, as I do many culinary mints, but where I want them, not where they want to go. The bee balm has a bed of its own near the vegetable garden, where several colors of it have a prominent place outside the fence on one boundary, blooming for weeks in July. The culinary types are relegated to a highly controlled location: beneath the spigots on the sides of the house. It is always a little bit shady there, and quite soggy (which they like), but they can't really go very far (the foundation of the house is inhospitable, and so is the stone patio—though they keep rooting under the pavers anyway). They disguise the plumbing nicely, and there is always the pleasure of their scent when I go to start the water running and brush against them.

Artemisia includes a number of unruly plants, but oh, those silvery gray leaves. The variegated goutweed (*Aegopodium podograria* 'Variegatum') is almost too easy to grow . . . a real weed. But I love it beneath the stand of pines along my roadside boundary, an attention-getting ground cover for shade.

Another shade-tolerant ground cover, yellow archangel (*Lamiastrum galeobdolon*) has vinelike runners and silver-splashed leaves, with bright yellow flowers in spring. It will gladly spill over a low wall or simply carpet the ground, like an ivy, and is pretty easy to rip out when the time comes.

ABOVE **The giant leaves of *Petasites* seem about to engulf the shed.** RIGHT **Columbines in the front garden.**
FOLLOWING PAGES **Bee balm through the seasons. *Ajuga* blooms in front of a cairn of upside-down flowerpots.**

Plain old rhubarb (*Rheum palmatum*) is unkill-able, I suspect, and with its giant mass of leaves and statuesque flower stalks, one feels quite proud to have grown it. So is 5-foot-high comfrey (*Symphytum officinale*), a favorite of the bees when its blue flowers appear in late spring and summer. Even when I dig them out, the bits of thickened underground roots—almost woody masses—seem to leave behind enough to sprout another bumper crop, often many feet away. The comfrey travels sideways in every direction; the rhubarb is less aggressive. Both will grow in shade (and in the compost heap, by the way), and even if they're a bit too enthusiastic, they are to be admired for their energy.

As I look out the window, I am reminded of many more shot-in-the-arm types from the early days: *Ajuga,* for instance, and the low-growing sedums. And what about the giant of ground covers, *Petasites japonicus*? Fuki, as it is called in Japan, has umbrella-size, tropical-looking leaves and spreads like crazy,

particularly in moist and partly shaded areas, where it is happiest. It will run right out into the lawn, so be aware. When I was a beginning gardener, its perfor-mance made me proud, and even now I couldn't live without it (and will never have to). Like any aggres-sive plant, it must be managed—not allowed to wan-der from the space assigned. Remember who carries the shovel in the family (a hint: not the plant).

Having recommended such plants for their ease, I must add a caveat: You will spend the advanced-beginner phase of your gardening lifetime digging these plants out. I think it's worth it, because, after all, they offered the positive reinforcement required to stick at a hobby as demanding as gardening. If you start with the notorious finicky characters like del-phiniums and alpines, how far will your gardening career go? And here's a suggestion: Pass the out-casts to a neighbor who's looking a bit undone by fussy hybrid tea roses and the endless ritual of annual bedding out.

Adulthood

I give up. Enough is enough. I've had it. These are the kind of phrases, tired but true, on my mind by sundown each of these days, when latest spring has slipped into the reality of summer, after 8 or 10 hours spent trying to solve the puzzle I started in the dirt some years ago.

Where do all the plants go to make a pretty garden? I wonder, close to tears, surrounded by pots and pots of this and that. At the nursery, I had been certain I had to have them; now, in their company, I am feeling kind of lost.

What goes next to what? How many of these with how many of those will make the picture perfect? And why did I put that *there*, what was I *thinking?* Oh, why didn't I draw a plan, the way I tell others to do, and then stick to it? If only it were a jigsaw puzzle of cut-up cardboard pieces, and there was in each plant a clue—an interlocking edge that fit it into place and let you know you'd got it right. But that is not how it is, as anyone who has tried designing even a single flower bed will certainly confirm. The purple asters look good with the purple-leaved heuchera, and the allium is good spiking up through the artemisia, but those were merely good guesses— there are plenty of bad guesses, too. No wonder gardening is accomplished on one's knees.

My love-hate of garden making had been running perilously close to the dark side lately as I desperately dug and dug some more, determined to find the answer. But then came early June, and not-so-early June, and I was still out there, searching for the "right" arrangement. If I moved the smoke-bush one more time, or that poor, peripatetic pulmonaria, I would surely self-destruct. A weekend or two ago, I felt certain I could dig no more.

"If only I could plant everything in alphabetical rows, instead of trying to make it look good, I'd be off the hook," I whined to a friend.

"There is no hook," the wiser gardener replied, performing horticultural phone therapy. "You *created* the hook." That sounded very clever, and quite important, so I filed the remark carefully in my head. His garden is a showplace; he must know what he's talking about, I figured.

But I did not really understand his words until the following weekend, back in the dirt. I found myself feeling stressed and panicky, starting 10 tasks and finishing none, fixating on all the holes in the puzzle all over again. Then I was overcome by a wild, freeing thought: how liberating it would be to borrow the neighbor's tractor and mow the whole place to stubble! If there had been a helpline for suicidal gardeners, I would have called it. Oh, if only there was a Gardeners Anonymous.

Yes, the hook is my doing, and I had hung myself on it, by my nasty habit of seeing only the problems, the weak spots, the areas in need of tinkering. Perfectionism and starting a garden do not mix, I learned at that moment. My half-empty mentality gave no gold stars for what had been accomplished, only demerits for what had not.

If I created the hook, then it is my prerogative to unhook myself, yes? I am therefore declaring this Throw-in-the-Trowel Week, a horticultural holiday I heartily recommend that any other gardened-out souls adopt in their localities, too.

Admit it; spring is not just aging, it is past. So I say enough, and quickly set about to fill in any really embarrassing bare spots with annuals, or even pumpkin vines (where my puzzle's weaknesses were on a grander scale). An even layer of mulch can work miracles in uniting plants that have far from knit together, too, and a cleanly cut edge around the bed makes things look almost bearable. After these touches, only maintenance will be allowed until fall, when planting (hopefully without panic) may be permitted again.

Conveniently, it is especially good timing for such a declaration. The first official day of summer and the onset of consistently hot weather (hard on transplants and transplanters) have been marked. Time to plug in the last babies and crawl into the hammock with a glass of iced tea. Time to give it— the seedlings, the soil, the soul—a rest.

From this freshly liberated perspective, I think back upon my panic as if it were years in the past.

"All I seem to be doing is moving the same things around," I recall saying to the same wise friend.

"Well, then you are learning the secrets," he said, ever inscrutable.

And so I'll swing awhile and think of what I'll be able to move to where when the time comes, when the weather cools again and I am feeling refreshed, too.

Gardening is a process. Even great gardens don't start out great; they take time, and lots of reshuffling, the kind of thing we're all out there doing from early spring through right about now. *Gardening is a process.* I repeat this new mantra to myself now as I find myself with time to take a walk or watch the birds. Or—dare I say it?—with time to simply look at what I have accomplished.

Then I was overcome by a wild, freeing thought: how liberating it would be to borrow
the neighbor's tractor and mow the whole place to stubble!

SUCCESSION PLANTING OF VEGETABLES I sometimes think that no vegetable-garden plot would be big enough for my ambitions. But it's amazing what you can cram into your garden if you use every opportunity as it comes along. When I used to plant only once in the spring and then just sit back waiting for the summertime harvest, I reaped only a fraction of what I do now that I make subsequent sowings of many crops. This tactic, called succession

planting, can double or triple what you harvest from the same amount of space. If you want more than zucchinis and tomatoes in fall, keep planting now.

Midsummer is a key moment in the succession-planting scheme, when taking action can yield harvests of crops continuing right through frost—of fresh vegetables that would otherwise be only distant memories. When you pull the exhausted first row of bush beans, then Chinese cabbage, kale, or turnips could fill the space (assuming you have subsequent bean sowings already going—otherwise, plant some more beans). Carrots and beets and Swiss chard can be sown through July, for me, and radishes even later, so have seed on hand to plug into empty spaces. Likewise with salad crops: spinach, for instance, which likes cool weather, performs well again from a late-summer sowing, as does arugula, which I grow all summer but which bolts faster in the heat.

Peas can be sown again now for a fall harvest, but the second crop never seems as productive, frankly. Since the weather at the season's end can cool things down to a standstill in September some years, or nearer to November in others, it is hard to calculate whether a slower plant like peas will work when the climatic future is unknown. I try them in July anyway, because even moderate success is worth it.

Whatever the crop sown at this seasonal midpoint, be sure to give it the best chance by selecting a variety with a faster maturity date than you might care about in spring. Smaller carrots such as 'Thumbelina' are faster to develop, so you'll get more of them from a later planting than with full-size roots. Likewise, shorter bush peas like 'Novella' are better suited to a July sowing than the taller, later kinds I like in spring, and they are also easy to drape with a blanket overnight in case of early frost. The nonvining beans called bush beans, not tall pole beans, are best geared to second harvests; for extra-cold-tolerant radishes and lettuce, look for types with the word *winter* in the catalog or packet description. 'Rouge d'Hiver' lettuce (the French name of which translates as "red of winter") is one good choice.

Whether in midsummer or earlier, making room for a whole orderly row of something is unnecessary: a few square feet where a broccoli plant tuckered out could become home to more than a dozen lettuce or spinach plants, twice that many carrots or beets, a couple of cabbages, or some radicchio. If you use the space where broccoli raab or the first lettuce gives out for your eggplants or peppers or tomatoes, you're already practicing succession planting.

In late June or early July, I often direct-sow another hill of cucumbers and summer squash, since these later plants will fare better in the fall than the tired earlier ones, which may also have met their demise thanks to squash vine borers or other nuisances, which affect late sowings less. And although onions are one of the early transplants to the vegetable garden, by mail-ordering the ones geared to harsh winters—called hardy bunching onions—I can put in a crop in August, too.

As if this weren't enough to reap, I have another yield-enhancing tactic: a portable cold frame, about 5 feet long and 3 feet wide, that I perch on top of whatever space comes available for the latest salad and spinach sowings of all. I can harvest right up to the most brutal weather, or have spinach starting again in April from a fall sowing under the protection.

GROUND COVERS

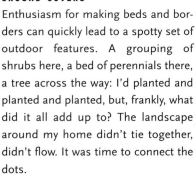

Enthusiasm for making beds and borders can quickly lead to a spotty set of outdoor features. A grouping of shrubs here, a bed of perennials there, a tree across the way: I'd planted and planted and planted, but, frankly, what did it all add up to? The landscape around my home didn't tie together, didn't flow. It was time to connect the dots.

This is what the plants we label ground covers do best: unite elements that otherwise look like so many disconnected islands. Ground covers pull the landscape together just the way that some manner of carpeting pulls together a room. And they don't have to be pachysandra, myrtle, or ivy to do the job well.

Almost any plant—from a shrub to ornamental grass to a vine to the tiniest, ground-hugging moss—can be used as a ground cover, if it is planted in mass or combined into a large area with other, similar-scale plants. But generally speaking, the most successful ground cover is a fairly low-growing plant that fills in fairly quickly to create a continuous cover—the underplanting, or ground level of a design, which may have many layers above it, up to large trees.

ABOVE *Tiarella cordifolia,* or foamflower, is a flowering native ground cover for shady spots of the garden.
OPPOSITE **A bluebird house in the upper field.**

Ground covers also serve other purposes in the garden. They act as a living mulch, reducing weeding and shading the soil beneath, which also benefits the shrubs or trees above them, who enjoy the cooler, moister root run. By doing this, ground covers can reduce watering requirements to far less than they would be if the soil were left bare. They can camouflage the ripening foliage of springtime bulbs interplanted within them (an excellent way to use bulbs, in fact, to extend the seasonal interest of the planting). They can prevent erosion, especially on banks, and substitute for lawn—reducing the wasted time, fuel, and money spent on lawn care. (There is no other ground cover as durable to foot traffic as lawn, however, and for that reason and others, it's by far the most-used ground cover of all.) Ground covers can carpet areas that are too steep or bumpy or too shady to grow grass on or to mow. They can also camouflage harsh edges here and there: the corner of a porch or the hard edges of a driveway can be blurred a bit by a drift of ground covers.

The difficult part of using ground covers is selecting one. I prefer planting them as mosaics rather than monochromes—a few textures and colors combined in each mass, with a big sweep of each plant, not one here and one there in spots. Some have become indispensable, and I turn to them again and again now that I have my own supply of so many good ones (once a planting is established, it always produces extras).

My favorites include *Tiarella cordifolia,* or foamflower, which has oak- or maple-shaped leaves that in the best varieties are a gleaming yellow-green or even marked in maroon. Foamflower, a small-scale but fast-growing native American woodland plant, sends up short wands of pinkish cream flowers in spring that last and last. *Lamium maculatum* 'White Nancy' is especially showy, its strongly marked leaves close to white; its flowers are also white. It is only 6 inches high or so and is tolerant of shady spots where there is ample soil moisture. Cut it back after flowering if it looks messy, and a fresh crop of leaves will follow. Barrenwort (*Epimedium*) will tolerate dry shade—no small challenge—as can some *Rodgersia*, which on a different scale altogether have very large, bold leaves.

The small version of goatsbeard, *Aruncus aethusifolius*, is compact and ferny and bears attractive creamy flowers that resemble astilbes. A grassy-textured choice that, like the *Aruncus*, will take a variety of light conditions is *Liriope*, or lilyturf, which is even evergreen in most zones (though it gets tattered by winter's end, at which point it, epimedium, and any others that have suffered should be sheared off and allowed to regrow). There are evergreen and deciduous ornamental gingers, including *Asarum europaeum*, which produces shiny heart-shaped foliage that persists into the cold months, and the larger *A. canadense*, a deciduous native. Neither one is related to the tropical plant whose root we eat as a spice—that's in the genus *Zingiber* (another example of why common names are so very useless).

There are many attractive ornamental grasses to choose from now as well as a growing selection of handsome grasslike plants called sedges (*Carex* species), including some gold-leaved forms, that bear investigation. Even hostas can be used as ground cover, as can astilbes (especially 'Sprite' and *A. chinensis* 'Pumila').

Let me see; what have I left out? There are low-growing sedums, and *Heuchera*, and bearberry (*Arctostaphylos uva-ursi*), and ajuga, and variegated ribbon grass (*Phalaris arundinacea* 'Picta'), and did I forget to mention ferns?

One of the most memorable ground-cover plantings I ever saw, in fact, was of ferns, in the woodland at ancient Powis Castle in Wales. As I came upon the glade, it looked as if the ferns were bursting into flower (which, of course, ferns do not do, since they predate the evolution of flowering plants). In fact, it was a colony of species lilies interplanted in the mass of ferns, a memorable sight indeed.

MEADOW PLANTS, MOWING STRATEGIES

I'd been mowing a couple of acres regularly for years when I suddenly had one of those ah-ha moments, realizing how many hours of my life and how many gallons of fuel I had wasted. Allowing the grass to grow to field height around the house wasn't in the cards, but in the outer areas I was ready for a change.

The hilly acre above the backyard—my primary view from the dining-room table and also from the outdoor space we use the most—was a prime target for rethinking. I had visited Madison, Wisconsin, where some forward-thinking gardeners time their mowings to encourage prairie-like meadows instead of close-cropped lawns, and I had also traveled to England, where selective mowing is an art form that

JUNE

THE UPPER FIELD AS THE MONTHS PASS

OCTOBER

NOVEMBER

complements the more formal beds and borders of many of the finest gardens. The sensual texture of unmown grass against the cropped green paths cut through it invite movement through the landscape.

But what would sprout on my hillside if I stopped thwarting it with the mower's blade? The first step in deciding not to mow, or rather when to selectively mow, is an evaluation of the plants already making their home in the area under consideration. Unless you're already a grass, weed, and wildflower expert, getting to know the backyard's natural wonders will require a set of guidebooks to each of those three categories, geared to your local area.

I let a section of my field grow in one summer to see what came up. I was able to identify a lot of remnants of agricultural crops—grasses that had been grown to feed the animals who once lived in my little barn, I suppose. There was a bit of yarrow (*Achillea millefolium,* not a native plant but a common alien), hints of goldenrod (*Solidago* species, a late-blooming native wildflower), butter-and-eggs (*Linaria*), some grasslike sedges (*Carex* species), and an orange-flowered hawkweed (*Hieracium* species). There were also a few clumps of a grass I had seen in many of those Wisconsin prairie garden: little bluestem (*Andropogon scoparius* or *Schizachyrium scoparium*), a prairie native whose range extends all the way to the East Coast. This became my target species: the one I'd coddle and favor above the others, the one I'd design my mowing strategy around.

Now I mow the hilly acre above the backyard only once a year, in late May, when the undesirable cool-season plants I don't want (fodder-type grasses that are remnants of farming days gone by) are already well up and growing. The mowing must be timed just before the awakening of the warm-season native little bluestem that I wish to encourage. By lopping off the growth of the unwanted early starters, I give the bluestem (and along with it other late starters) an edge. In just four years of once-a-season mowing, I went from having a few stray clumps of the bluestem

in an acre to about 30 percent coverage. Some years, I may mow twice, if a lot of messy debris was left behind by winter. Then I'll mow as early as I can in spring, and again at the moment already described.

An unexpected benefit of this kind of mowing—besides the time savings—is seeing what other plants vie for a leading role in my little meadow. One year the yarrow seemed to take over in midsummer, and I was concerned—should I pull it out, I wondered? But the next summer it played only a supporting role, while the goldenrods took center stage through fall.

My meadow is a miniature lesson in succession—the natural order of what follows what when humans stop messing with it. It reminds me that the land in my region was once all wooded and was cleared by humans to build their houses, to provide their firewood, and so on. My mowings are, of course, a form of tinkering, but I forgive myself by thinking that they simulate the effects of fires that once were allowed to occur periodically, or were even encouraged a bit by Native American peoples, who saw the benefits the fires provided by favoring grasses that the game animals they hunted liked to graze over the woody plants. My mowing, provided I also rake up the debris vigorously, is like a fire.

I am already noticing the primary lesson about succession in any field or meadow in my region: it tries very hard to revert to a woodland if allowed to do so. Young woody plants find their way in, beginning with some brambles and succeeded by young trees and such, which if left unchecked will quickly change the complexion of things altogether.

If you have a large area of grass, try mowing it less and enjoying it more.

CUTBACKS

Is there life after heatstroke? I always wonder that after a few of summer's prolonged blasts of 90-plus degrees. Both plants and gardener are well on their way to withering, or at least they look that way.

Here is where a good haircut and a tall drink can help both garden and gardener. In early August, I realize that if I don't act, the garden will just peter out, months before the first hint of frost. Some annuals that have been in place for a couple of months have grown leggy; many perennials beg for their faded flowers to be removed. The garden has a bad case of what a friend calls "the shaggies"—unwanted frowsiness that makes it look a mess.

The solution: Take to the garden with shears and be ruthless. At the very least, the payoff for midsummer cutbacks will be a tidier garden. At best, there will be some reblooms, too. The plants and you will feel much better afterward. I always hack back catmint (*Nepeta*) and any of my artemisia that flowered, taking them down about two-thirds of the way to the ground. Pulmonarias, too, are looking ratty by now and will regrow quickly after a drastic summer haircut. Most of the mints like a stern hand, including bee balm (when it finishes flowering) and the traditional culinary kinds. Lopsided plants in containers likewise get a cutback, particularly the so-called annuals like petunias. Even cosmos, which have grown so tall that they are out of scale with everything, will respond to being cut in half with a fuller, second wave of bloom through frost, as will ageratum and many others.

Once you have performed your barber's tasks, the drink follows. Make it a long, deep one, since this is typically a hot and dry time of year. Lace it with a shot of soluble liquid fertilizer, diluted according to package directions, to get the plants growing again.

DIVIDING IRISES

The general rule on when to divide perennials is this: Divide spring bloomers in fall, fall bloomers in spring. This strategy is geared to avoiding losing a season of bloom, or at least minimize the loss. If you don't care about that, divide them at either time, so long as it's when the soil is moist and the weather is relatively cool, to ease stress.

Cutting back *Nicotiana sylvestris* to encourage another round of bloom.

And then come the exceptions, the plants that actually like to be divided in midsummer. Daylilies, for example, are typically divided after bloom, in mid- to late summer, although they are so durable that they could probably be divided anytime and not miss a beat. And mid-July through September is when the bearded-iris specialists dig and ship their crops, and that's a hint that it's a good time for dividing yours.

Overgrown bearded irises will not flower well. To divide and rejuvenate a planting, gently dig up the old clumps and then use a knife to cut away the oldest part in the center—the part without leaves jutting upward from it. What you will be left with are pieces with leaves, and some will be doubles (shaped like a Y, with a fan of foliage growing from the upper points of the Y) and other singles (straight pieces with a set of leaves at just one end). Replant these pieces in circular or triangular groups with the leafy ends pointing outward (away from the center of the circle or triangle). If they are spaced about 8 to 15 inches apart (closer with the small pieces, farther apart with the large ones), they will need dividing only every three to four years.

Sometimes the whole planting doesn't need to be dug up. Simply cutting out the old, withered por-

ABOVE **Irises beside the vegetable-garden fence.** BELOW RIGHT **The odd yellow flowers of *Phlomis russeliana* in a jumble of *Clematis recta* and ribbon grass.** BELOW LEFT **Sedum and see-through *Verbena bonariensis*.**

tions with a knife will make room for the more vigorous bits of rhizome, which can be left right in place.

Acid soil is anathema to bearded irises, so give them a dose of lime each year if your soil is acidic. Don't feed them lots of nitrogen; it promotes soft tissue that's prone to rot. Rock phosphate, superphosphate, or bonemeal is preferred; sprinkle a dusting over the planting in very early spring or very late fall. Too much water in summer can also soften the rhizomes; let them bake, not drown, and they'll be much happier. Never plant the rhizomes completely underground, since their fat little bodies like to sun themselves and should be left partly exposed. And don't cut off iris foliage that looks healthy (it's some odd tradition to do so after the plants flower, or when they're being moved). Unless it's spotted or withered, leave it on the plant as long as you can. The more photosynthesis the plant is able to manage, the more energy it will have for flowering next year.

WEAVERS AND SEE-THROUGHS

A woman—a professional gardener—visited a renowned public garden known for its effusive plantings and unexpected combinations. Upon returning home, her boss asked her how she had enjoyed the place. "I didn't really like the way that all the plants touched," she said, having missed the point.

In a good, established garden, no plant is an island (and the mulch isn't meant to be the focal point). Many gardeners would offer money to make the plants touch faster, rather than waiting from two or three to five years or even longer for that "mature" or "filled-in" look a garden gets if you stick with it. I am one of them.

One class of plants that help make this happen a little faster—and a lot more romantically—are known to expert gardeners as weavers. Weavers are the plants whose natural habit is to reach out and touch their neighbors, or even wrap their arms around them. I immediately think of baby's breath (*Gypsophila paniculata*) when I think of weavers, and of some of the cloudlike, low to medium-height asters, like the heath aster (*Aster ericoides*) and its cousin *A. lateriflorus horizontalis*. Such asters are among my favorite weavers because by the time they flower, in fall, something is really needed to tie the tired pieces of the garden together.

Knautia macedonica is another weaver, as is *Aster* × *frikartii*—not because either one has tiny, cloudlike flowers (they are both large, and crimson and lavender-blue, respectively) but because they are inclined to flop here and there and marry with other plants in an appealing way. Some of the looser perennial geraniums (like *Geranium asphodeloides*, some forms of *G.* × *oxonianum*, *G. procurrens*, and *G. wallichianum* 'Buxton's Variety') are weavers, and so are the shorter-stature clematis, such as *Clematis recta*, which scramble happily through the other inhabitants of a perennial bed or shrubbery.

Another class of plants named for their habit are sometimes called the see-throughs: plants that take up little room on ground level but instead give an airy appearance up above. Tall verbena (*Verbena bonariensis*) is a classic see-through (it is a self-sowing annual in my climate, but it overwinters in warmer zones). Its tall, wiry stems seem to come up out of nowhere, holding up clusters of tiny purple flowers that make ideal landing pads for colorful butterflies. It blooms from midsummer until hard frost for me, from hefty nursery seedlings set out in May; self-sowns start their bloom later. Many of the tall alliums, or ornamental onions, are like that: virtually no mass at ground level, with spectacular blooms on high that seem to float in midair. Horsetail (*Equisetum*) is another great see-through. Yes, I know it's invasive. But managed by a stern hand each spring, it can be kept in bounds, and few such handy plants are more linear and architectural.

FOLIAGE, THE GARDEN'S WARDROBE

I bristle when I see those charts of perennials or shrubs where they list just the name, height, bloom time, and flower color the plant comes in. Why isn't there a box in the chart about the plant's leaves?

Flowers alone do not a garden make. Since they represent the reproductive portion of the plant's life cycle, they are merely a moment in its year. Many flowers last only a couple of weeks, tops, while the season may go on for six months.

Even in the most common leaf color, green, the range of shades is infinite, from nearly chartreuse to olive, gray, and blue, with countless midgreen tones in between. Add to that the diversity of leaf size, shape, and texture, and you start to get the picture. Then take it one step further, to plants with variegated leaves (whether splashed or striped or edged with white, silver or gold, pink or red), and on to red-leaved plants and yellow-leaved ones, too.

Many gardeners, especially beginners, are afraid of showy leaves, particularly unusually colored ones, because they aren't sure of what goes with what. Green is the garden's neutral, and seems safe, but too much plain old leaf green is pure monotony. The plume poppy (*Macleaya cordata*), a very tall perennial, knows this. To avoid being boring, it shows off its leaves' pure white undersides whenever the wind rustles them. Look for plants that have this something extra.

Two designer friends who rely heavily on colorful-leaved plants explain their strategy this way: To make colorful-leaved plants work in a design, you have to have several "incidents" using them around the yard. Don't just go out and buy a purple-leaved or golden shrub and stick it alone somewhere; tie it into the larger picture by repeating the motif with an underplanting of coordinating purple-leaved perennials (*Heuchera,* for instance, and the dark-leaved *Cimicifuga atropurpurea* 'Brunette') or gold ones (like golden hostas; grasses; or creeping Jenny, *Lysimachia nummularia* 'Aurea'). Then in the not-too-distant background, repeat the motif once more, with a small tree in the same general color. When viewing the garden, the eye will be drawn across the scene from one incident to the next, instead of just focusing on the single out-of-place oddball.

Colorful-leaved plants can play important tricks with perspective and light, too. Golden-leaved plants and white-variegated ones advance, making dark corners pop; dark-leaved shrubs tend to recede, giving a sense of distance even in a tight space. They also make an exciting foil for flowers (try purple flowers, such as a clematis, draped over a golden-leaved shrub, or a bright-colored annual vine like canary creeper, *Tropaeolum peregrinum,* over a purple barberry). Use these special plants to your advantage.

Whatever color the foliage, a plant's leaves

should also be evaluated for the ornamentality of their texture and shape, because these qualities, too, can be used to great advantage in designing gardens. If you put ferns, astilbes, and dwarf goatsbeard (*Aruncus aethusifolius*) all next to one another, it wouldn't set off their individual beauties—it would just read as a mass of ferny-textured leaves. But one of those near a hosta, with its large, bold leaves, and something spiky or very vertical alongside that—a grass or an iris, for instance—would be a lot more interesting. Very large leaved plants, like the red-leaved castor bean (*Ricinus communis* 'Carmencita') or *Astilboides tabularis* (formerly *Rodgersia tabularis*), could be an exciting addition to a design, and they are underutilized, I think, probably because people are afraid of anything so out of the ordinary scale-wise. Remember that there are no mistakes in gardening, just experiments with a variety of outcomes —some more pleasing than others, but every one a critical bit of education.

PUMPKINS AND SQUASH

I do not know where my special affinity for pumpkins and squash began, for I am no great fan of trick-or-treat and jack-o'-lanterns. But I admit being reduced each year to child age when I tap their giant seeds out of the packet or later on move among their giant

leaves to count the big fruits forming on the vine. At harvest time, I cannot wait to finally hug the off-spring, to cradle a well-grown Hubbard in the crook of my arm as if it were my own flesh (if somewhat thicker, sweeter, and more vividly colored).

The best pumpkins and squash have another endearing quality: they'll stick around on the kitchen counter until you're ready for them, rather than melt into a sloppy mess of spoiled fruit the way a tomato does. The so-called good keepers — thick-fleshed ones like cheese pumpkins or butternut squash— will last all winter in storage. And they are versatile ingredients: a base for soup, a mashed vegetable, the stuff of pies or cakes, or even pureed and folded into the batter of biscuits.

Although the genus *Cucurbita* is a bit of a tangle, like a field of pumpkin vines, the ones we grow most commonly fit into one of four species, all natives of Central to South America. The summer squash, which are usually eaten immature, before their skins harden, all fit into the popular species *C. pepo,* as do some popular winter squash like 'Delicata', 'Acorn', and 'Sweet Dumpling'. Tiny pumpkins like 'Jack Be Little' and 'Little Boo' (white-skinned) are also off-spring of this species, as are sugar pumpkins and the kind we grow for carving at Halloween.

The best keepers are in the species *C. moschata,* and these have the sweetest flesh, usually dark orange in color. This is where 'Butternut', 'Canada Crookneck', and the cheese pumpkins (so called because their shape is somewhat flattened, like a wheel of cheese) fit in. *C. maxima* includes the plant kingdom's largest fruits—the contest winners approaching half a ton—as well as many other out-standing varieties for eating, like 'Kabocha', 'Rouge Vif d'Etampes', and the Hokkaido and Hubbard types. The least-grown species is *C. argyrosperma,* which tends to want a hotter summer than I can offer, but I have succeeded occasionally with one

A tag-sale wheelbarrow with squash and pumpkins from the vegetable garden at harvest time.

LEFT **Smokebush going extra-colorful in fall.** RIGHT
The gaudy leaves of Hottuynia cordata 'Chameleon'.

of its outstanding members, 'Green-Striped Cushaw'.

Good cooking texture and taste are not attributes of the thin-walled, stringy jack-o'-lanterns, whose flesh is also watery and doesn't last . . . carve them, yes, but grow their cousins as food-stuffs. Look for descriptions such as "thick-fleshed," "fine-grained," and "good keeper" in the seed catalogs if you want to make a pie—a Hubbard, for instance, or a cushaw will do quite beautifully, much more deliciously than 'Small Sugar' or the other traditional pie pumpkins.

The best pumpkins I ever grew were done this way: In early May, I stretched black plastic sheeting over a bed to which I had first added more than 6 inches of rotted cow manure. After about three weeks of letting the sun heat up the plastic-covered soil, I cut X's in the sheeting every 5 feet in each direction. Into each X, I poked a few seeds of a different variety, along with a large wooden label to identify them. I watered the seeds, and that was it. So long as the weather or hose provided regular, deep soakings, the plants were basically carefree, though I will admit to tossing the vines over the garden fence as they grew, and in one case up a nearby pine tree limb, to give them more room to spread out. Larger fruit can be had by thinning to one or at most two fruits per vine, but I am not out for contest entries— merely for sweet, vitamin-rich food, and a bit of companionship (thankfully, the kind that is delightfully quirky, and nice to look at, but doesn't talk back).

SEEING RED, ETC.

Although red-leaved maples and barberries, bronzy crab apples, and purple-leaved plum trees are almost stereotypes, I am surprised that more gardeners haven't caught on to the value of perennials with the same colors of foliage, from bright red to smoky purple to coppery bronze. Even when they are not in bloom, plants with reddish foliage make an important contribution to the garden picture.

Several native perennials, including a wine-leaved *Lysimachia ciliata, Penstemon digitalis* 'Husker Red', and the many purple-leaved *Heuchera* (such as 'Palace Purple', 'Montrose Purple', and 'Garnet'), are plants I rely on for rich leaf color all growing season long. So are some flashy aliens, like various bugle-weeds (*Ajuga* species) and sedums. Among the latter are many good choices: *Sedum* 'Mohrchen', *S. telephium* 'Munstead Red', *S.* 'Vera Jameson', and *S.* 'Ruby Glow', to name just a few, have leaves from deep maroon to purple-green to bluish pink. Many sedums are also bone-hardy, are easy to propagate, and seem to grow almost without help of any kind (though not in soggy soil or in complete shade). The sempervivums (*Sempervivum* species), another succulent, can be had with reddish foliage, too.

Surveying the yard quickly, I notice in a partly shady area the handsome *Ligularia dentata* 'Desdemona', with purplish foliage and chrome yellow daisylike flowers in late summer, and *Cimicifuga atropurpurea* 'Brunette', a purple-leaved fall bloomer. The vegetable garden boasts some very ornamental red-leaved lettuces, which would make nice (if temporary) edging for a flower border, and the purple of cabbages and some kales, plus purple basil and shiso (*Perilla frutescens*, or beefsteak plant, the herb

Even when they are not in bloom, plants with reddish foliage make an important contribution to the garden picture.

used to color vinegars in Japanese cuisine and thereby make pickled ginger turn pink). Elsewhere, there is a wine-colored canna and a dahlia with similarly purple-red foliage to offer as suggestions, along with some bronze-leaved astilbes and purple-leaved lobelia hybrids such as 'Queen Victoria' (not nearly hardy for me, but possible as an annual).

Poor, dear *Coleus* has had a stigma against it, but if you get away from the jarring seed mixtures into the named varieties, which are finally reaching nurseries and catalogs, there are maroon to purple-red plants to be had, and shade-tolerant ones at that.

Few plants are truly red. Probably the reddest ones are Japanese blood grass, *Imperata cylindrica* 'Red Baron', and the red-, yellow-, and green-splashed chameleon plant, *Houttuynia cordata* 'Chameleon'. Both of these ground covers can be invasive where they are comfortable, so beware. The hardy begonia (*Begonia grandis*), like many indoor begonias, has red undersides to its foliage, and it is somewhat better mannered, though it will seed itself around in the shady spots it likes.

OREGANO AND ITS COUSINS

I wanted to plant oregano, as I expect many gardeners do, for a fresh supply to cook with. That may sound like a simple desire, although fulfilling it was anything but. The plant marked simply as "Oregano" at the garden center grew lush with little care, a low, green mound with a pleasant aroma if touched. But come harvest time, the oregano leaves tasted like peppery dirt, if that good, and the plant had spread in every direction I did not intend for it. Not exactly what I had had in mind for a seasoning with my homegrown tomatoes, or a good garden subject.

Was it poor (or too-rich) soil? The wrong location? Improper care?

Wrong plant.

Called "the mystery plant of the herb world" by

LEFT **Globe thistle, bee balm, and sedum in a vase.**

The Rodale Herb Book, "oregano" is the common name for a small multitude of plants that are mostly useless in the kitchen. Among them are many true oreganos, in the genus *Origanum,* and also many plants that aren't. Mexican oregano (*Lippia graveolens*) is a relative of lemon verbena, not oregano. Cuban oregano (*Coleus amboinicus*) is a succulent that tastes and smells like oregano and makes a good houseplant. It is used like oregano in Cuban cuisine. Italian oregano thyme, a member of the genus *Thymus,* also has the familiar oregano scent.

Among the true oreganos, there are choices for great beauty, such as *O. vulgare* 'Aureum', a golden-leaved form. (My sorry plant was probably just plain *O. vulgare*—not even pretty like the golden kind.) Sweet marjoram, a kind of oregano known as *O. majorana,* is more the stuff of French cuisine and is an excellent culinary herb. Pot marjoram, *O. onites,* is also savory-flavored.

But if you want to cook with the classic oregano taste, you'll probably want Greek oregano, *O. heracleoticum,* which is a pungent species and one of the best for strong, true oregano taste, as is seedless oregano, *O. viride.* The true oreganos will be most flavorful just before the flowers open, when the maximum concentration of oils is in the leaves. Bunch sprigs together with a rubber band and hang them in a dark, dry place to dry, or use fresh.

ANNUAL VINES

In the absence of grand architecture—substantial trees and shrubs and other elements that would combine to qualify as a garden's "bones"—$10 worth of annual-vine seeds will go a long way toward coherence. There is no faster way to make it look as if you have been gardening a space awhile than to get some height into the picture.

Makeshift supports can be fashioned by anyone —no carpentry experience required—from monofilament, string, wire and hook-eyes, or metal or plastic mesh. Quickly erected tripods and tepees—three- or four-legged affairs of tree limbs or long, thick bamboo canes—will also by midsummer be covered by foliage and then flowers that will continue until hard frost takes them down.

Among the morning glories alone are enough choices to suit any color scheme. Catalogs such as those from The Fragrant Path and Select Seeds/ Antique Flowers (see Sources) have especially good lists of these and other old-fashioned annual vines, many of which can be direct-sown where they are to grow, once the soil has warmed. Morning glories (*Ipomoea purpurea*), moonflower (*I. alba*), purple hyacinth beans (*Dolichos lablab*), and scarlet runner beans (*Phaseolus coccineus*) are easily handled this way (be sure to soak the morning-glory seeds overnight first), as are the many wacky ornamental gourds, whose beautiful white flowers are followed by every manner of odd-looking fruit.

A few slower growers must be started indoors extra-early, or the yield will be only foliage before frost ends the season. Cup-and-saucer vine (*Cobaea scandens*) and purple bell vine (*Rhodochiton atrosanguineum*) are two examples. And the faster starters benefit from this extra coddling, too, since plants set out after frost will have a jump of many weeks.

Other annual vines I recommend trying from seed include variegated Japanese hops (*Humulus japonicus* 'Variegatus'), which produces white-splashed foliage, and *Mina lobata,* which has beautiful leaves and odd flowers that look like tiny multicolored pennants hanging on a line. In the genus *Asarina,* there are a few good annual vines of a delicate texture, and I also have a fondness for the blue-green leaves and golden flowers of the canary-bird creeper, *Tropaeolum peregrinum.*

Perhaps the most endearing annual vine of all is called love-in-a-puff or balloon vine (*Cardiospermum halicacabum*). It is a delightful chartreuse froth of tendrils and delicate leaves, punctuated from midsummer on by an increasing supply of semiopaque bright green balloons (the puffs), inside which form large seeds with a single heart etched on each one (the love). A friend had it self-sow in his asparagus patch, where the combination of fresh greens and soft textures of the vine and the ripening asparagus fronds is positively electric.

TALL PERENNIALS

In the way that I like the botanical extravagance of outsize leaves, I also have a strong affinity for plants that attain a great height in a single season. Although in my first years of gardening I would not have known what to do with a 6- or 8-foot perennial, today I can think of many things: to create a seasonal living wall or screen; to back a perennial border; to punctuate the corners of a bed or the start of a path, the way a column might; or merely to break up the monotony of a bed of so many 2- and 3-footers with a giant exclamation point.

And one more thing: I can use them to simply cause wonder, since even after these many seasons among the giants of the garden, I never fail to be astonished when I have to look up into their faces.

Six-foot-plus perennials like Joe Pye weed (*Eupatorium purpureum*), meadow rue (*Thalictrum rochebrunianum*), giant coneflower (*Rudbeckia nitida* 'Herbstsonne'), and the invasive but beautiful plume poppy (*Macleaya cordata*) come into their season in midsummer and deserve a space in every sunny garden. Be sure to site the latter where the lovely white undersides of its leaves can be seen rustling in the breeze. Bugbane (*Cimicifuga racemosa*), which can top 8 feet with its creamy bottlebrush flowers, will manage in sun or partial shade. New York ironweed (*Vernonia noveboracensis*) is another towering possibility. It bears magenta-purple flowers in fall, and there are many large asters to enrich the picture.

ABOVE RIGHT **Gourds clamber up and onto a panel of wire fencing.** ABOVE LEFT + BELOW **Joe Pye weed in the late-summer garden, and in a vase with** *Angelica gigas, Tithonia rotundifolia,* **and** *Ligularia* **'Desdemona'.**

RASPBERRIES

One summer, in a year when the precipitation exceeded the annual average by more than 10 inches, I found out how to grow raspberries properly: water them a lot. I suppose this is true of most fruiting plants, but because the bramble fruits are so much like the roadside weeds that are their cousins, I guess I had expected them to get along on their own water-wise, and had been stingy.

Fruit also likes plenty of sun to ripen, and raspberries are no exception.

Other than my old apple trees, plus some wild elderberries (*Sambucus*) that I grow along my property line and pick for making jam, the only fruits I regularly grow are raspberries. My reason is simple: even when they are in season (in July and again in September in my area), they are fairly expensive, and I figure it's good value for my garden space.

There are many named varieties of raspberries to choose from, and they fall into two categories: ones that bear once each season, and others (called everbearing) that fruit twice.

How you manage the raspberry plot each year will also dictate when and how much your bushes yield. **1** In March, they look like an overgrown thicket. My neighbor simply mows his canes to the ground every year in late winter, minimizing any early harvest and fostering more fruit later on.

2 I prefer to be a bit less aggressive, and instead I spend one of the first sunny March or April days cutting out all the canes that fruited the previous year right to the ground.

3 I also reduce all the others by one-third to one-half. (Technically, I should have removed the finished canes right after the July harvest ended, but I rarely get to it at that time.)

4 Old canes and dead ones (which along with damaged ones should be taken out anytime they occur) are easy to tell apart from vigorous younger ones by the color of their bark. Instead of a warm, orange-brown, the undesirable canes will usually be gray or white, peeling or wobbly.

5 Right after pruning and cleanup in earliest spring I give the raspberries a dose of all-natural organic fertilizer and mulch them well to thwart weeds. A weedy raspberry patch will not be a productive one.

When first planted, my raspberries were the proper $2^1/_2$ feet apart in the rows, with 4 to 5 feet between rows. But in the well-prepared soil, to which I added lots of leaf mold and other composts, they quickly filled in via their prodigious network of suckers. I pull up any suckers that move outside the width of the row into the path, and I simply let new shoots fill the gaps where old canes have been cut out.

At harvest time, the key is to pick regularly, since these fruits are not as durable as apples and pears. If there is no time to make jam or if there are too many to eat fresh, I simply toss them into zipper-lock bags in the freezer, to be cooked up later into a sauce or jam or simpy enjoyed over ice cream.

Senescence

"The plant is dead, Margaret, you jerk. Oh, that's just great, you killed the poor thing." If anyone but the woodpeckers was listening, that is how they would hear me talking to myself in the garden more than I care to admit, whenever another plant bites the dust.

The year's body count to date: a total of six dead, including two of three 'Powis Castle' artemisias (I don't wonder so much why two died, but why one of these marginally hardy things lived for me); two roses; a South African perennial called *Phygelius* that I was supposed to lift and carry indoors for the winter but forgot; and a thyme tucked into the front walk that never rebounded after suffering regular, repeated blows from the snow shovel. *Mea culpa,* times six. Back from the dead (or, more correctly, back after a long absence underground): the chameleon plant (*Houttuynia cordata*), a variegated ground cover with flashy green, yellow, and red leaves. It poked through the soil surface around late July, after a shocking nine-month absence. Talk about a long winter's nap.

Gone missing, presumed dead: 24 *Camassia,* bulbs in the lily family that are supposed to produce spikes of blue flowers in spring, and 8 hardy *Cyclamen* corms I set out last fall. ("What did you expect?" a cyclamen-savvy fellow gardener said when I expressed my assumption of failure. "You plant them in the fall, they go dormant, and if you're lucky they bloom the next August, then make leaves, and then the whole process repeats itself." Stay tuned—no sightings yet.)

There are so many ways to kill a plant, it's a wonder any of us has a garden at all. You can underwater or overwater it to death; starve it into a deep and deadly faint or overfeed it so it gets soft and floppy and too weak to survive. You can fry it in too much sun, or torture it in too-deep shade so that it stretches up and out toward the light and grows thin and spindly in the process, then finally falls down dead. You can permit a fast-growing thug of a plant to run a better-mannered one right over, instead of jumping in (playing God of the Garden) and moving one of them.

"Some plants just melt away—like the wicked witch," a friend says, describing the cause of loss in his garden. "They get smothered by another plant, and too moist, and they just disappear."

Sometimes, of course, it is just "the weather" that kills a plant that's in your care. "The weather" makes a highly serviceable euphemism for when you don't know what did the poor thing in. There's always some aberrant pattern in recent memory to hark back to, and other gardeners will nod their heads empathically about how they, too, suffered through the deluge/drought/heat/freeze.

Or here's another refuge for those who know full well they've committed an act of floracide: "It wasn't hardy for me." Meaning I killed it, but it was the plant's fault for not being tough enough.

Bugs and diseases are another culprit, and while the gardener is responsible for keeping such disas-

ters under control whenever possible (but without chemicals, please), again these can be labeled bigger-than-thou situations. You're practically blameless against Japanese beetles, or gypsy moths, or mealybugs.

Then there's the really violent stuff. Like when you overprune a shrub or tree until it sprouts no more, or transplant something one too many times until the roots are mangled and the multiple shocks to its system are too great. Or how about this: you can step on a plant over and over again while working near it in a bed.

Now, although I would never go so far as to suggest ways to kill plants, I'd simply like to come out of the closet and say that it happens to every one of us, beginner to advanced. If fear of failure succeeds in making you shy, you will miss out, resigned instead to a life of mere marigolds. (Or silk and plastic plant substitutes, if the risk of murder takes on major phobic proportions.)

Think about it this way—those who don't at least try to grow things will never have the chance to utter the words of a true veteran: "Been there, killed that."

So what if they are finicky or even unreliable? I, for one, am running right out to buy some delphiniums, and some red-hot pokers—the orange and yellow torch lilies properly known as *Kniphofia* that I didn't know how to use when I first tried them 20 years ago but now look just right. And I'm going to plant them together and coax them into simultaneous bloom (yes, true blue with blazing orange—I'm feeling wild at the moment).

If I succeed, I'll feel fantastic; if they flop, I'll use in a vase the few miserable blooms I do get.

And if they just downright die, I'll make the best of a bad situation and buy something else to fill their places. Perhaps another round of the same two challenges, because the only way to figure some plants out is to kill a couple of generations until you get it right or fail for good and certain.

The death of a plant is an opportunity, smarter gardeners are always telling me; focus not on the loss but on the room it opens up.

"Was it pushed, or did it jump? Or was it just a case of neglect?" a friend who's new to gardening says teasingly when she hears that the topic at hand is dead plants, touching on another important point. Perhaps we unconsciously nudge some of our less beloved plants toward the grave. As hard as it is to thin carrot seedlings—killing babies, yes, but an essential act if any at all of the siblings are to survive and reach full potential—it is harder still to toss out a full-grown perennial or shrub simply because it does not thrill and delight you.

This is when murder is completely premeditated—and completely forgivable.

"*Do it,*" says a wiser gardening friend, who actually delights in days spent culling the collection of plants in his care for those that just don't measure up. "*Toss them.* It will make you a better gardener."

GRASSES Much is said and written about plants that look good, or smell good, but less so about ones that sound good. The ornamental grasses, particularly the larger-scale ones, make beautiful music. I have come to depend on the rustling of a particularly giant *Miscanthus sinensis* whose varietal name I do not know, which in moist years (or when I remember to water it) easily

reaches 10 feet. Against a corner of the house, it is at the ready from midsummer through at least midwinter to make itself known on breezy days, and I eagerly listen for it. The variety 'Goliath' is one good, very tall *M. sinensis* that would suit this purpose.

So would the giant reed (*Arundo donax*), though in Zone 5 it is not winter-hardy the way the *Miscanthus* is. I would have to grow it in a whiskey barrel or other large planter, then haul it into the basement to lie quiet and cool all winter long. With the variegated form, *A.d.* 'Variegata', if not the plain green one, it would be well worth the hauling to have what looks like a creamy-variegated bamboo in the garden all summer long.

Grasses are so beautiful in fall and winter that I leave them standing, and then as spring approaches I either mow, cut, or burn the tattered foliage down (burning is legal in my agricultural community; get a permit, or don't burn). If the winter is not too wet, which can flatten the grasses early, their warm tones and movement will be a welcome sight in the worst of months, and the birds appreciate the seeds.

As a contrast to an acre of meadow above the house I mow just once or twice a year, where I am encouraging native little bluestem grass, I planted a 20-foot-wide island of various variegated *Miscanthus*. Ornamental grasses of large scale can be set out in single clumps, for emphasis, or massed to create a

CLOCKWISE FROM TOP LEFT **Miscanthus sinensis in flower. A detail of the 'Zebrinus' form of M. sinensis. Phalaris arundinacea 'Picta'. The seed heads of Chasmanthium latifolium.**

whole wall. Use them to screen out the functional parts of the yard—the compost heap, for instance, or the parking area—or to create a sense of garden rooms, dividing one area from another for much of the year.

Less architectural but no less beautiful are some of the smaller grasses, particularly northern sea oats (*Chasmanthium latifolium*), which reaches about 30 inches high, and variegated purple moor grass (*Molinia caerulea* 'Variegata'), just half that size. The former (a native American) creates an arching mound of nice green foliage all summer, in sun or part shade, and then forms its fantastic flattened seed heads—like a cross section of a pinecone, for want of a better description—that turn from green to coppery shades in fall. They are extremely long-lasting in dried arrangements. The purple moor grass is a tidy mound of creamy striped foliage all season, well suited for the front of a bed.

There are many fine varieties in the genus *Pennisetum*, known as fountain grass, but unfortunately my favorites can't survive my Zone 5 winters —so I grow them as annuals or in pots. The red-leaved ones, in particular, such as *P. setaceum* 'Rubrum', are fine in containers or borders.

A final grass I would not garden without is ribbon grass, or variegated gardener's garters, *Phalaris arundinacea* 'Picta'. Though a notorious spreader, especially where soil moisture is ample, it makes up for bad behavior with clean, white-striped foliage that provides a showy foil for white *Narcissus* 'Thalia' underplanted in the grass or for the white blooms of nearby *Clematis recta* a little later in the show. Since it can take shade, it's a useful tool for lightening dark spaces, and remember: the plant doesn't have the shovel, you do. Keeping it in line is easy if you pay attention and dig out runners spring and fall.

AUTUMN-INTEREST PLANTS

The growing season may come alive in earliest spring in colors suited to a baby's layette—pastels of yellow, blue, and white—but when the end is near, the best gardens go out in a true blaze of glory. Bring on the color, in leaf and flower. Don't go softly.

Until I began to add fall-interest plants to my repertory, "if only" and "what if" and "what might have been"—regret-laden terminology— was all I had to say about the garden starting around mid-August, when many spring and summer stars have the look of aging divas. The garden was burned out, not burning hot with color.

Yes, there was *Sedum* 'Autumn Joy', a perennial that rightly has earned a place in many gardens lately. And a few ornamental grasses—some variegated *Miscanthus,* mostly—were beginning to do their thing. But autumn can be so much more than just a couple of isolated spots of color. It can be a whole extra season in the garden, which even in my cold climate means extending the enjoyment for about two months each year.

Besides the visual treat, planning for a full fall season in the landscape includes enhancing the attractiveness of your garden to wildlife. If you plant with them in mind, they will drop in for a look at the hot-colored leaves like tourists do on New England's autumn weekends; the additional supply of pollen, nectar, seeds, and fruit at a time when at least the first two are getting in short supply means that butterflies, in particular, are likely to make your garden a regular hangout. Especially if you resist the urge to

tidy up too fast, and let every last drop of pollen and every last seed head come to fruition.

Like a design staged to peak at any other season, a fall garden depends on many layers of plants, from trees to shrubs, perennials, bulbs, and ground covers. When making a garden, include a good dose of fall-interest trees and shrubs among those that make up the backbone of the landscape, things like fothergilla (almost nothing holds its orange and red and yellow leaves longer), double-file (*Viburnum plicatum tomentosum*) and the American cranberry bush (*V. trilobum*), cutleaf staghorn sumac (*Rhus typhina* 'Laciniata'), *Hydrangea paniculata* 'Grandiflora', winged euonymus (*Euonymus alatus*), oakleaf hydrangea (*Hydrangea quercifolia*), blueberries (*Vaccinium corymbosum*), spicebush (*Lindera benzoin*), and Virginia sweetspire (*Itea virginica* 'Henry's Garnet'). Red-leaved shrubs like smokebush (*Cotinus coggygria* 'Purpurea') and sand cherry (*Prunus cistena*) just get hotter looking as fall advances, as does even the lowliest form of barberry (*Berberis thunbergii*). Some of the deciduous azaleas, including *Rhododendron viscosum, R. vaseyi,* and best of all *R. schlippenbachii,* also called the royal azalea, color up well in fall. Among small trees, the Asian *Stewartia pseudocamellia* and many of the dogwoods (*Cornus kousa,* for instance, and native *C. florida*), are known for excellent fall color, and so is the native tree called sourwood (*Oxydendrum arboreum*), one of the most brilliant. Other fiery candidates include the parrot tree (*Parrotia persica*), *Franklinia alatamaha,* some hawthorns (*Crataegus phaenopyrum* and *C. viridis*), and Japanese maple (*Acer palmatum*).

Some easy vines, like Boston ivy and Virginia creeper, both members of the genus *Parthenocissus,* heat up in fall, too, and make a startling backdrop for herbaceous plants like asters and autumn crocus (*Colchicum*), whose peak color coincides.

Fruiting plants, from deciduous hollies to vi-

LEFT **A nonhardy salvia grown as an annual.**
RIGHT **The peegee hydrangea in its glory.**

burnums to beautyberry (*Callicarpa* species), are a mainstay of the autumnal show (many of them are covered elsewhere under their genus; the longest-lasting ones are discussed on page 159).

A gardener wanting good results at this time of year must bone up on the following perennials and bulbs or bulblike plants, at the very minimum: toad lily (*Tricyrtis* species), *Kirengeshoma palmata*, asters, ironweed (*Vernonia*), bush clover (*Lespedeza thunbergii*), hybrid Japanese anemones (*Anemone japonica* and *A.* × *hybrida*), goldenrod (*Solidago*), *Solidaster*, *Salvia*, *Canna*, and *Dahlia*. The first two and the anemone are perfectly happy in part shade.

Although not grown for their fall interest expressly, silver-leaved artemisias and lamb's ears are another much-appreciated plant at this time of year. Their cool, silvery blue color sets off the warm tones of fall expertly. Likewise, the honey-gold stage that marks the last breath of many ferns and hostas is one of their best moments, poised just before they fade in a glorious, violently colored decline to sleep awhile until the cycle begins again.

SILVER AND GRAY LEAVES

More than any other plants I grow, the silver-leaved ones seem to manage to keep their cool look while standing up to heat, drought, and the other stresses of an advancing season without a complaint. Even though they are of the color usually associated with aging, they always look fresh and new to me. And as a foil for flower colors, they are outstanding.

Lamb's ears (*Stachys byzantina*) is an essential in my garden, and I even enjoy the odd flower stems it sends up in summer (as do the bees), although many gardeners cut them off as they develop or grow the infrequent-flowering forms instead. The variety 'Big Ears', for instance, has extra-large leaves and flowers less than the straight species. So does

'Countess Helene Von Stein'. Whichever one you grow, expect a fuzzy, silver mat of leaves ideally suited to corners and edges of the flower border, as an underplanting for old roses, or as a ground cover in some other sunny, well-drained site.

Salvia argentea (*argentea* being the adjective meaning "silver" in Latin) is a biennial or short-lived perennial producing basal rosettes of silvery white foliage its first year, then pushing up a flower stalk the next. The Scotch thistle, *Onopordum acanthium*, is a tall gray-silver presence, as is the artichoke relative called cardoon (*Cynara cardunculus*), which I cannot overwinter outdoors but enjoy nonetheless as an ornamental annual. The genus *Verbascum* (the mulleins) also includes a number of grayish silver biennials with large leaves at the base and a spiky flower stalk as they mature. And there is even a silvery-leaved fern: *Athyrium goeringianum* 'Pictum', the Japanese painted fern.

The genus *Artemisia* probably has more silvery plants in it than almost any other. Unfortunately, some well-known artemisias (such as *A. ludoviciana* 'Silver Queen') are notorious land hogs that run sideways in every direction, without a shred of respect for their neighbors. I planted a whole island of it once, however, at a significant distance from the house, with no other inhabitant but some of the tall, large-flowered purple alliums like *Allium giganteum*. Even from afar I could enjoy the show of those two high-drama plants, and the island became a focal point of the late-spring to summer landscape, drawing the eye past the yard into the fields beyond.

One plant in the genus that could be used as edging is a selection of Asian beach wormwood, *Artemisia stelleriana*, called 'Silver Brocade', and it is particularly well suited to a sandy soil. It forms mats of foliage. Perhaps the most appropriate to garden usage, however, are tidy artemisias like 'Powis Castle', named for the compelling garden in Wales

ABOVE LEFT **An assortment of salvia flowers.**
RIGHT **Other gleanings of the fading season.**

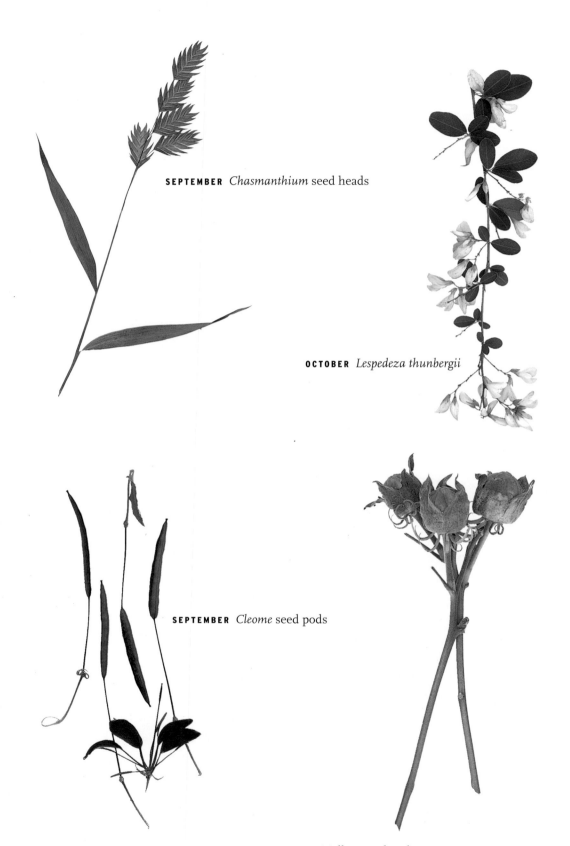

SEPTEMBER *Chasmanthium* seed heads

OCTOBER *Lespedeza thunbergii*

SEPTEMBER *Cleome* seed pods

OCTOBER Mallow seed pods

where it grows even in dry, poor pockets of soil on preposterously terraced cliffsides. These artemisias' habit is more that of a small shrub—mounds a couple to several feet wide and high. I cherish my few aging, shrubby plants of plain old wormwood, *A. absinthium*, which I cut back hard when they flower in summer, as is the practice with the flowering artemisias. Even better forms are 'Lambrook Silver' or 'Huntington', which have finely textured foliage.

For silver of a different sort altogether, try certain ghostly members of the genus *Eryngium,* such as Miss Willmott's ghost (*E. giganteum*) or the native American rattlesnake master (*E. yuccifolium*), which at first inspection might be confused with some kind of teasel or thistle. There are many blue-flowered species, too, some with grayish silver foliage, commonly termed the sea hollies (though many are sadly tender). Pushing up through dark-leaved purple barberries or in a sea of hot-pink rose campion (*Lychnis coronaria*), or wherever else they seed themselves, the various *Eryngium* are spectacular metallic accents to the garden.

LEFT **Lamb's ears with bees.** RIGHT *Salvia argentea* **foliage.** OPPOSITE **Heading out to plant alliums.**

BULB PLANTING

Much has been said earlier about particular kinds of bulbs to choose from and how to grow them (see "Odd Minor Bulbs," chapter 2), but this is the time of year for it, and so a few miscellaneous reminders are called for. First, almost across the board, the larger the bulb the better—the extra cost is worth it, unless you are in no hurry for results. Order by mail, and early (July ordering is better, even, than now and may qualify you for discounts). Don't buy bulbs in the garden center if you can avoid it, since they are expensive, and the selection is limited. Garden-center bulbs are often packed in bags of 6 or 10, which fosters spotty planting. The catalogs sell by 25s, 50s, and 100s, which is more like it for achieving any impact. And don't be put off by inexpensive "minor" (small-scale) bulbs; typically all that means is that these are good choices for beginners, because they are easy to grow and multiply fast—hence their lower price.

Whatever kind of bulb you're planting, see if it is possible to extend the season of bloom by incorporating more than one species or variety into a design (for early, midseason, and late bloom within that plant's total possible period of flowering). With daffodils, tulips, lilies, and crocuses, among others, this is possible, and it means a more interesting garden over more weeks.

A final caveat: Do not shop from bulb companies that collect their supplies from the wild. Carefully read the catalog policy statement—which any reputable company should print—and if it's not clear, call and ask where they get their bulbs. The words you are looking for are "nursery-propagated," meaning started and finished in the nursery, not "nursery-grown," which can mean that the bulbs were wild-collected and then grown on awhile in the nursery, which isn't good enough to protect wild populations of these precious plants. They continue to be under the threat of extinction in their native haunts, and gardeners must help keep them there.

TAKING INVENTORY

Resolutions are meant to be made on New Year's Eve, but for a gardener that is no time for such important business. As the garden begins its inexorable decline toward the season's end, it is time to take note of how things fared—before it's all cleaned up and erased from memory, or masked by a blanket of snow.

After spring, this is when the garden-journal entries are most frequent—noting which plants didn't fare well (with suspicions why), which are too crowded, and which look too isolated (add some more of the same) or too overpowering (subtract) for the garden's good.

Besides such practicalities, fall is probably the best time to evaluate and record your own failures, too. Did you expect too much of yourself—order too heavily, or shop too often? (A clear indication of over-

shopping is a small army of plants in nursery pots still sitting in the driveway.) Was there simply too much deadheading, watering, and weeding to manage? Would such troubles be alleviated by a helper (or weed-thwarting mulch, or landscape fabric topped by mulch in some areas, or a drip-irrigation system you could install now)? Should you find someone to mow next year to free up more time for real gardening, or at least buy a riding mower (usually on sale in fall) to speed the process? Were there too many tomatoes and cucumbers to eat or can (or worse, too few)?

Before the catalogs arrive in early winter, record your observations. The temptation will be too great once the mailbox starts to fill up, with all those plants and seeds calling out to be ordered, and repeats of the same troubles will be harder to resist.

GARLIC

Although it is sold alongside the asparagus roots, strawberry plants, and seed potatoes in the nurseries each spring, April or May is no time to plant garlic. October is.

Garlic cloves planted in the fall will be ready for harvest the following summer, around July, and will be more than worth the wait. Garlic is best ordered in the spring from Filaree Farms, Southern Exposure Seed Exchange, or another catalog with a diverse list (see Sources), for fall shipment; if you did not order any but want to plant it now, simply purchase the freshest heads you can find from a greengrocer and use those as your starter stock this year. The advantage of ordering from a specialty catalog is the selection: Filaree, for instance, has hundreds of distinct varieties. Generally, the silver-skin kinds are the most familiar, like most store-bought garlic, and are good keepers. But many less long-lasting kinds are also more delicious as well as quite beautiful, with reddish- or purple-skinned cloves.

Many people are passionate about elephant garlic: they either love or hate it. Actually, botanically it isn't a garlic at all but a kind of leek, although it is cultivated the same way as its cousins the true garlics. Because the bulbs are larger, plant them deeper and snip off the flower head when it forms.

Garlic is easy to grow. Simply separate the bulbs (heads) into individual cloves, and set them in the ground so that a few inches of soil covers the tip of each clove. In warm zones, 1½ inches deep is fine; in cold-winter areas, 3 to 4 inches is more like it. Space the cloves about 6 inches apart in all directions. The cloves should be oriented to point upward—that is, the part that was the basal plate, where the roots were attached, should be at the bottom of the hole. Experts recommend using the smallest and very largest cloves for eating, and planting the biggest of the medium-size ones, which yield the best.

They also assert that because garlic is propagated by division, not grown from seed, you must give the plant time to adjust to its new home in your soil. The first year's crop may not be great, but go ahead and continue the process, replanting from your crop.

The bulbs will begin to grow roots, sometimes also sending up green shoots before winter, and in my cold zone I mulch them once the tops stop growing, after a hard freeze that begins to solidify the ground, to keep them from heaving during thaws.

A fairly neutral soil, about pH 6.5 to 7, is desirable, as is a spot in full sun. The soil should be fertile; I work in lots of compost, well-rotted manure, phosphorus (in the form of rock phosphate), and potassium (in the form of greensand).

In spring, when the greens are growing again, feed with fish emulsion, but withhold fertilizer later on, since too much nitrogen can promote rot. Keep the row well weeded, and if flowers are produced, snip them off. Don't let garlic dry out while it's actively growing; mulch lightly.

Perhaps the most important step of all is proper harvesting and curing. Harvesting should be done just as the foliage begins to yellow, not after it dries up completely and falls over. Carefully dig the bulbs and move them to a spot out of the sun that is warm, dry, and ventilated, where they can sit undisturbed for at least a month. Wire racks are great for this purpose, because they allow lots of air to circulate. Cut the stems off when the bulbs are well cured, using pruning shears to snip them an inch above the bulb.

As mentioned above, some of the cured garlic can be used as the basis of next year's crop and replanted in fall. I also pot up a number of cloves each fall in windowsill containers for "garlic greens" all winter.

LEFT **Globe thistle by the bed-frame rose trellis.**
RIGHT **Elephant garlic cloves.** FAR RIGHT **Typical garlic.**

MAKING A GARDEN POND

No effort on my part as a gardener has done more to encourage wildlife in the garden than the digging of two small water gardens. Although I grow many wildlife-friendly plants, it is water that everybody seems to delight in most—from the various species of dragonflies and damselflies that regularly mate and breed now in my backyard, to the birds who bathe and drink here (including a flock of wild turkeys), to every kind of frog listed for my region in the regional wildlife guidebooks. If you build it, they will come—snakes, toads, salamanders, even a weasel, whom I have caught drinking from the pond's edge on occasion.

The hardest part of making a water garden is digging a large enough hole. My first pond was the result of moving a large shrub—I never bought topsoil to backfill the hole its uprooting left, and I finally got so sick of the crater in the backyard that I decided to dig out some more, line the hole with rubber, and add water. Any location is fine, so long as it is sunny enough for aquatic plants.

Although water-garden books and catalogs usually recommend 18 inches as the desired pond depth, in a frost-prone area like mine that shallow a pool would freeze solid, killing any fish or frogs that lived in it. The first time out, I didn't understand this problem. 1 The following November, on the brink of frozen fish, I had an even deeper hole created nearby—one about 3 feet deep. It still requires what is called a pond deicer (an electric device, from water-garden supply catalogs, that resembles a floating hotplate) to prevent a solid sheet of ice from forming and suffocating the fish, since gas exchange cannot occur under a sheet of solid ice. The device is inexpensive (perhaps $40); the electricity to run it is not. My fish may have cost only $2 apiece or less at the pet store, but I have become oddly attached to them.

It is just one of the many expenses I gladly meet for these newest members of my garden community, but even if I didn't want to shell out for fish food, water conditioners, and so forth, I would still have water gardens. The sound of moving water alone is worth the work and the cost.

One of the biggest expenses is the liner, made either of a pre-formed plastic or fiberglass shell or of heavy-gauge flexible plastic or rubber sheeting (usually about 45 mil thick). The advantage of the sheeting is that you can deter-mine any shape of pool you want. You will also need some kind of underliner—either a special fabric made for the purpose from a water-garden supplier or merely some castoff rugs—to buffer the liner from any roots or rocks; some sand to make a base at the pool bottom, beneath the under-liner; and basic garden tools (a long-handled shovel, a pry bar for dislodging rocks, a square shovel for cutting clean edges, a long level, and a piece of 2 x 4 long enough to span the opening and check that the opposite and adja-cent sides are level with one another).

The shape of a pond can be free-form (design it right on the ground with rope or a garden hose) or more formal and sym-metrical (mark it off with stakes and line). If you want to grow shallow-water plants—bog crea-tures such as pitcher plants (*Sarracenia* species)—or if you want an extra-deep layer of stone edging (called coping) so that the liner and water are below ground level, you'll need to dig not just

the inner, main hole but also a shallower shelf all the way around (or only partway around if you only want a small shelf for a few plants). Mark off the perimeter of the shelf and of the hole itself inside that, and begin by digging the hole first. The walls of the hole should not be straight up and down but should slant back slightly. Remember to dig deeper than your desired pool depth to accommodate the sand layer (from 2 to 6 inches deep) you'll put on the bottom.

2 Once the hole is excavated, begin on the shelf, which typically can be a foot or so wide and deep, depending on your design and coping plans. Again, slant the edges slightly back.

Next remove any stones that protrude into the hole or shelf, and cut any tree roots, too, that could damage the liner. Use the board and the level to ascertain that the sides are all plumb. Dump the sand in the bottom, level it with a 2 x 4 dragged across the surface, and install the underliner. The liner comes next. Where the fabric is too ample for the space, the liner (or under-liner) must be carefully tucked or folded until a good fit is attained. Do not cut the extra from the edges yet.

3 First fill the liner with water to stretch it down into place, then

drain the pond and install your coping (whether bricks, stones, or pavers), with the liner tucked beneath the coping material.

4 + 5 Look at the coping stones from every angle to make sure they are pleasingly arranged.

Before refilling the pond, install the plumbing, but note that this is, in my experience, where things get confusing. How strong a pump you'll need to do what you want to do ornamentally and practically is one issue; the other is what kind of filtration will best suit your needs. When a water garden includes fish, the issue of filtration (and aeration of the water) becomes very important, and the less expensive filters (mechanical ones that simply trap the dirt in sponges, mesh, or other screens) require frequent attention. The so-called biological

RIGHT **The tools of the pond maker's trade—pruner, mat knife, X-Acto knife, and special hammer for splitting stone.**

filters are large exterior tubs in which a combination of mechanical and biological action (thanks to friendly bacteria that build up and process wastes) occurs. The biological filter for my 1,700-gallon pond, for instance, is the size of a dishwasher lying on end —not easy to disguise, but ever so easy to maintain, requiring only occasional draining by opening a valve to flush excess wastes. Compared with the mechanical filter attached to the pump in my 700-gallon pool, it costs many times as much (perhaps $500 compared to $50).

A small waterfall can be run effectively with an inexpensive pump, but if you plan to move water uphill over any distance before it returns on its own back down to the pond **(6 + 7)** things start to get expensive. Ask the supplier you're ordering from to help you compute which pump size is right for what you want to do, after measuring carefully the distance from the pond surface to the top of the proposed falls.

Where to position the pump is another challenge, particularly in a shallow pond, since it can be neither directly on the bottom (it will suck up too much debris) nor

too high in the water (it will show, and it won't effectively circulate all the water through it). It also needs to be at the opposite end from the return (whether a waterfall, fountain, or mere pipe), so that you aren't recirculating the same water again and again.

I lifted my pump off the floor of the pond with a few bricks and a large, flat-topped stone and then erected a concealing device for the pump above that from two cinder blocks topped with a rectangular slab of slate from the stone yard. Some combination of bricks, slate, and cinder blocks will make a good platform for your pump, though alkaline material leaching from the blocks may alter pH and harm fish and plants. A regular pH test is essential, and corrective solution (from a water-garden supplier or the pet store) should be used as indicated. Another trick: A vegetable dye sold by suppliers will make the water a safe but inky black color, showing off your fish while disguising plumbing parts.

8 To further beautify the pond, we later built a small patio around it. **9** But in the winter it's hard to see anything but the heater and open water. We really

miss the moving water and the green of the water plants.

Come spring, we buy fresh plants each year, both floating and submerged ones, and remove the nonhardy ones each fall after frost. Getting the submerged plants in the pool as early in spring as they are available is important, because it can help balance the pond community and thwart an algae bloom.

Shading the water with floating plants also helps keep algae under control (one-third to two-thirds of the surface should be covered), because it deprives the algae of sunlight. Moving water from a fountain or waterfall is likewise somewhat beneficial, and mechanical removal (with your hands, a net, or a pool skimmer) also is advised. I have also had success with adding noniodized salt (the kosher or pickling kinds only, because iodine would hurt the fish). Noniodized salt, at the rate of up to $2^{1}/_{2}$ pounds per 100 gallons of water, will not only kill algae, it will also act as a tonic for weak or stressed-out fish. Dilute the salt in buckets of water and add it gradually around the pond surface, not all at once in one spot.

Many wild asters, representing numerous species, pop up around my garden and the surrounding fields

ASTERS

I still recall the suspicious glare of the person beside me in the checkout line at the garden center a few springs ago, when I was buying asters and she was buying azaleas. Her purchases were blooming. Mine looked dead. She was smug then, but at this time of year, I think it's pretty clear who got the better deal. Partly because they come so late in the season, and partly because they don't look like much until then, asters are one of the lessons usually learned late in a gardener's career.

Many wild asters, representing numerous species, pop up around my garden and the surrounding fields and roadsides, and even in the woods. The first aster to intentionally find a home with me, though, was 'Little Carlow', whose dime-size violet flowers are produced over many weeks in fall. I would not be without this plant. Another winner in the genus *Aster* is *A. lateriflorus horizontalis*, which carries sprays of tiny pale pink flowers on wide-spreading branches. It is one of the plants known as weavers, as is the species *A. ericoides*, or heath aster (see page 117). Thanks to plant nuts like Dan Hinkley of Heronswood Nursery near Seattle (see Sources), there are now more asters available to American gardeners than ever before—his catalog lists about 50, at last count.

Most asters bloom in fall, though there are summer bloomers, too. Among the autumn choices the range extends from late August to right up against hard frost, as late as November. Plan accordingly.

Conventional (read: English) wisdom says to lift your asters and divide them every year, but I think that can be extended to every three years without any ill effect. With the taller ones, in particular, it's advisable to pinch or prune them once or twice before letting them fill out and bloom, to ensure bushier, more compact plants. Dan Hinkley takes the easy approach to this and simply whacks back to about 6 inches from the ground all the tall varieties around the Fourth of July. Until lately, I let the deer do the job, and they were happy to cooperate, munching off the top half of the plants like clockwork every June, once the fawns were up and about after mating season and the herd was back on the move.

Asters are generally sun lovers, though *A. divaricatus* (the white wood aster) and *A. macrophyllus,* to name two, can handle shade. Like many of the asters, these are native American wildflowers, and they easily adapt to a busy gardener's inattention. The trick is to learn to tolerate their appearance, which ranges from nondescript to downright weedy, from late spring when they emerge through their glory moment, and there are a few strategies you can use to make this easier. First, site them in the company of other plants whose foliage is attention-getting (like artemisias or purple-leaved plants, for instance) to divert the gaze. Second, and perhaps better, plant them in a fall border that is not the main focus of the summer months, where they will happily mingle with coincidental bloomers like autumn crocus (*Colchicum*), Japanese hybrid anemones (*Anemone* × *hybrida* and *A. japonica*), goldenrods (*Solidago*), cannas, dahlias, and salvias, among other possibilities. In such a border, spring bulbs could be planted for another season of bloom, and then the attention could be focused elsewhere in June, July, and August, before the aster border steals the show.

Aster 'Little Carlow' will eventually cover itself with lavender-violet flowers.

and roadsides, and even in the woods.

LATE CLEMATIS

After a few deaths and disappearances by finicky, large-flowered clematis in the garden, probably due to the mysterious malady known as clematis wilt, I had about given up. Then I met the sweet autumn clematis, *Clematis maximowicziana* (formerly *C. paniculata*), which asked for little and gave a lot.

Its tiny, sweet-smelling, cream-colored flowers in September create a frothy mass, and the vigor of this plant just about ensures success. Here is a clematis to start with, one robust enough to form a canopy over a seating area, or cascade over a stone wall, or cover some unsightly body in the garden you haven't been able to bury yet—the skeleton of a dead small tree or large shrub, for instance, or the ubiquitous tree stump that thumbs its nose at the possibility of removal.

A number of other clematis, including *C. viticella*, which bears small, soft violet flowers, are similarly timed, and I am eager to try the little-grown *C. grata*, with its creamy white fall flowers, since it is reported to be very hardy, unlike many otherwise desirable clematis possibilities.

Even with the fussy ones, I eventually learned that there are some things you can do to offer clematis the best possible chance of peak performance, many of which involve the way you plant them in the first place, of course. For the most part, they like sun—at least five hours a day. There is an expression that they like their faces in the sun and their feet in the shade, which is true enough and actually quite easy to oblige. Simply plant ground covers at their base, or lay a slab of stone over their root system to keep the sun from baking them while leaving the soil beneath shaded, cool, and moist. Siting them on the north side of the tree or shrub they are meant to climb will also do the trick.

But that's getting ahead of ourselves. First dig a hole at least 1½ feet wide and deep (2 feet by 2 feet is better), and amend the excavated soil with leaf mold, well-aged compost, and some lime (assuming your

OPPOSITE **A mirrored seat in the woodland.** LEFT **Sweet autumn clematis beside a peegee hydrangea and a single *Nicotiana* seedling that was allowed to stay where it sowed itself.** RIGHT **An unnamed white clematis.**

soil is not already neutral or slightly alkaline, the way clematis like it). If the soil is heavy, a little sand may also be worked into the improved mixture. Position the clematis in the hole so that the crown is an inch below the soil surface, and backfill with the improved medium. Water well, and offer the vine some support to get it started on its vertical ascent—monofilament, wire, a trellis, brush, or a combination will do.

Eventually, there is the matter of pruning, which seems to unravel even many expert gardeners. The words of the great English gardener and writer Christopher Lloyd stand out in my mind whenever I panic, shears in hand, before a clematis vine. In his clematis book, he likened an unpruned clematis to a disemboweled mattress, and so I always think "Who wants their sprung bedsprings hanging on the trellis?" and just get on with it.

But first (and I am speaking of the vining kinds, not the shrubby ones) you have to know what kind you have: spring blooming, for instance, or summer-or-later blooming. Early bloomers flower on the previous year's wood, so pruning that off will eliminate flowers. Hence, once the plant has grown and filled in to create a framework of a pleasing size, prune the spring bloomers only when they're out of bounds, or misshapen, or to remove weak, damaged, dead, or overcrowded stems. Otherwise, simply cut back all the growth that just flowered, so the plant is back within the bounds of the framework. Do this within a month of flowering—the same basic rule you'd follow for a spring-blooming shrub like a lilac. *C. montana*, *C. alpina*, and *C. macropetala* are pruned this way; the last two are not as vigorous as the first, and therefore they are likely to need a lot less restraining with the shears. *C. montana* can also simply be given free range up into a tree or over a large pergola or arbor, where it can just grow and grow without pruning, if that suits your purpose.

Summer and autumn bloomers flower on new growth (like a peegee hydrangea does, for example, or a hybrid tea rose), so they can be pruned hard, down to the lowest pair of buds on each stem, which may be about a foot or so from the base. Do this in early spring, just after the buds swell. If they are not pruned, they become very sparse at the base and flower only where the new wood is, not below that point—an unbalanced, unattractive plant. Some examples are the cultivars in the *Viticella* and *Texensis* groups, as well as the familiar *C.* × *jackmanii*.

Then there are the clematis that try to confuse you, blooming on old and new wood both, meaning they have a show in spring and again in fall, basically. Pruning is optional with these. If you do prune them hard, they'll flower later in the season; if you leave them be, the show will start earlier. A general tidying up each year, after the final show, works fine for a while, but the plant eventually requires a hard pruning.

SAVING SEEDS

Seeds are forming everywhere at this time of year, a resource to be gathered in and preserved, a thread to tie together this year's garden and the next. Not all seeds will be worth saving, however, so I limit my efforts to species or open-pollinated (nonhybrid) plants that can be expected to come true from seed in subsequent generations.

Technically, in the best of worlds, the gardener would also save seed only from plants that had been kept segregated from other close cousins they were capable of breeding with, and that is particularly true among the squash and pumpkins, and tomatoes, to name two. Well, I simply don't have room for segregating plants, so I save the seeds anyhow.

There are two basic kinds of seeds—those that are moist and those that are dry. The former group—including tomatoes and pumpkins, two kinds I like to save—requires some extra attention; badly handled seed will rot or get moldy. There are more complicated ways to go about removing the pulp, but I simply wash the gloppy mess off in a strainer, and then I spread the remaining pumpkin, winter squash, or tomato pulp, seeds and all, out on a few thicknesses of paper toweling and leave them out to dry on the counter. Once they are well dried, I pick the seeds off the toweling (I've even just rolled up the dry toweling, seed side in, and stored it that way all winter, with good results). Dry seeds, such as from columbines or *Nicotiana*, can simply be emptied directly into a glassine envelope or a jar.

Whatever seed you save, be sure to wait until the plant is ready for you to have it: once it is fully ripened, and not before. The trick is to get the seed before the plant disperses it but not before it's ready. Seeds should be stored in a cool, dry, dark place in airtight containers—not where they will freeze, or bake, or get damp, please. Numerous envelopes of seeds can be stashed together in large glass jars. Spoon a few tablespoons of powdered milk into the bottom of the jars first, to soak up any moisture that might permeate the paper packets and harm the seeds. Untreated kitty litter—pure clay only, not that chemical-treated and scented stuff—would also work as a wicking agent.

Hostas are good right up until their last honey-colored moments in fall; don't clean up too soon.

Whatever seed you save, be sure to wait until the plant is ready for you to have it: once it is fully ripened, and not before. The trick is to get the seed before the plant disperses it but not before it's ready.

stable, but remember that unless they are well composted in a fast-decomposing (or "hot") pile, between 120 and 160 degrees Fahrenheit, they will be full of the seeds of what the animals were fed, so plan to let them rot thoroughly in a heap that's really cooking along. A compost thermometer will help eliminate the guesswork here.

If you want to use compost as a mulch later on, I recommend composting leaves separately, in their own pile. They can be shredded to speed up the process; simply rake them into small piles where the heap is to be made and run over them with the mower. Moisten the pile and perhaps sprinkle in some soil or old compost. The leaves can also be left whole, in bags or in a pile, all winter and then shredded come spring.

How often you turn your pile will affect the speed at which finished material is ready to be returned to the garden; if you've got time, you can escape turning and just let nature take its course. I turn twice a year, in spring and in late summer or fall, and extract the lowest layer, where the finished stuff is hiding. Before using the compost in the garden, I toss it through a homemade sifter, into a wheelbarrow, to cull the stones and sticks and unfinished bits like tenacious corncobs or thick roots.

GARDEN GHOSTS:
WHAT TO LEAVE STANDING ALL WINTER

Compulsive cleaning is one disorder I have escaped. The faded garden has too much valuable in it to be merely swept clean the moment hard frost hits. The spent garden is rich in information and also in wildlife food—precious resources that should not be squandered by a gardener in a hurry.

I leave many perennials standing through much of the winter—until they look lousy, basically. My criterion: If it has stout stems and holds some kind of seed head or fruit, it stays until it has nothing left to offer. What used to be known as composites— members of what is now called the aster family—are

particularly suitable, as are many grasses. The overwintering birds appreciate not just the seeds but also the thicket effect the tangle of spent plants creates, which buffets them from the wind and gives them momentary perches for their scouting trips around the yard in search of food.

A gardener friend in England says he leaves many perennials standing for another reason, more archaeological than environmental. In late winter, when he does, at last, clean up, he takes stock of what did well and what didn't. The plant debris leaves valuable clues: maybe the phlox wasn't as tall as last year, which is evident even from the dead stems, or maybe the iris had fewer flower stems than usual (and therefore fewer flowers). And if an ambitious plant is creeping into its neighbor and you cut down its stems now without correcting the situation, you won't remember the invasion until the trespasser is up and growing again next year. Looking for causes of disappointments or failures in late winter, before the problem repeats another season, is very valuable, because it is in late winter that he's mapping out his plan for what to divide, replant, or replace come spring.

The exceptions: diseased things, like peonies in a year plagued by the fungal disease botrytis, or pulmonaria leaves after a bad summer of powdery

Seed heads of black-eyed Susan, left, and bee balm are ornamental, and eventually used by the birds as food or perch. Leave them standing.

mildew. Cut those right to the ground and dispose of the leaves in the trash, not the compost. And there are some things that I never cut in fall, unless it's to remove dead branches. Among these are the so-called subshrubs, plants that are somewhere between perennials and shrubs—woody but also soft, like *Potentilla,* Russian sage (*Perovskia atriplicifo-lia*), and *Caryopteris.* All of these tend to suffer tip damage (or somewhat worse) in winter, so I let the winter have its way and then prune back to healthy tissue in early spring, rather than cutting back now and exposing even more of the subshrub to harm. Rosemary and lavender (if I could grow them well in my cold region) would fall into the same category; so do the many varieties of thyme.

There is one more reason to leave some of what I call "garden ghosts" up through at least part of the winter, and that's to ensure that you get a good crop of self-sowns (see "Editing Self-Sowns," chapter 3). Many late-to-ripen seed heads wouldn't have a chance to spread their progeny around if they were cut down and carried away in fall. I like to think it's the winter wind that spreads things around so artfully—better than I could ever position them—and so I give it a chance to do its thing, meanwhile lightening my workload just a little so I can plant some extra bulbs or rake the fallen leaves into a mulch pile instead.

COLD FRAMES AND OTHER SAFE HAVENS

Although a cold frame is a four-season tool, a great many of us think of it most at this time of year, when it serves as a place to tuck away marginally hardy things that need just a tiny bit more protection; to force pots of tulips and daffodils that need a chill period to bloom (see page 159); to protect young plants not quite ready for their first winter in the open ground; to grow an extra crop of salad, when the weather's too cold in the garden proper. But a cold frame is also a good place to harden off seedlings in spring or to root cuttings of shrubs in summer.

I have two kinds of frames: built-in wooden ones, with Plexiglas tops, that are dug about 1½ feet into the earth and extend another couple of feet or so aboveground at their highest point; and a portable aluminum frame with double-thick plastic panes, from a mail-order house. The advantage of the portable one is that it can be plopped down where it's needed, when it's needed, such as over the last salads in the garden at this time of year, or over a few rows of root vegetables to keep the ground beneath from freezing so I can dig them into early winter.

Beyond putting the cold frame to use, there are other wintertime tucking-in chores to attend to now, including mounding up the roses with soil and mulch after the ground begins to freeze. I pile about a foot of earth around their bases to insulate the graft union, where the desirable rose variety is attached to the more vigorous rootstock.

Mulch can be applied now to other areas of the garden, once the ground gets solid, but I don't bother with much of it except in newly planted areas and over the crowns of delicate things.

Nor do I wrap much of anything in burlap, but some broad-leaved and needled evergreens prone to windburn and sunscald in difficult winter spots will benefit from the added protection. Drive the stakes into the ground now, before the ground goes hard, and make a tent around the plants with the burlap, using a staple gun to attach it. If these plants are

A gardener friend in England says he leaves many

OPPOSITE **The frame of a portable cold frame (minus panels) ready to move into duty where needed.** ABOVE **A flock of wild turkeys is among many visitors to the backyard water gardens.**

kept well watered all summer and fall, right up to freezing, they will fare much better against the elements whether wrapped or not.

A friend grows *Gunnera manicata,* a very large-leaved perennial technically suited only to Zone 7 or warmer, in his Zone 5 garden, over the damp seep above his wastewater field. At hard frost, he lets the leaves fold down upon themselves, heaps the plant up with other leaves and straw, and then pops an upside-down whiskey barrel over the tucked-in gunner for the winter. It works. The same idea can be applied to tender fig trees (grow them up the side of the house near the chimney, where the ground never quite freezes, and wrap them with some kind of thick padding, like old quilts, and burlap tied on with rope). All of these methods are strictly trial and error; if you want to grow something badly, experiment.

WHAT TO SOW OUTDOORS NOW

The ground is getting crusty with frost, but before it becomes impenetrable, sow the spinach. Next spring, almost before it's possible to get out and sow the first seeds, there will be young plants already up and growing, and the harvest will be advanced by nearly a month. Spinach is so tough that even if it starts growing before winter, the tiny plants will hang on, growing a bit in thaw periods and then taking off in earliest spring. I have applied the same technique to arugula and even lettuce (look for cool-season kinds in this case), since when I have allowed these plants to go to seed one year in the vegetable garden, I've always had extra-early self-sown plants the next. Theoretically, now is the time to sow annual poppy seeds and those of love-in-a-mist (*Nigella damascena*), as well as larkspur (*Consolida ambigua*).

perennials standing for another reason, more archaeological than environmental.
In late winter, when he does, at last, clean up, he takes stock of what did well and what didn't.

BEAUTIFUL BARK

Though the beauty of a white-skinned birch against a snowy landscape is a classic winter image—the stuff of Christmas cards—many gardeners forget to shop for the quality of bark when they choose their trees. This is part of the job of creating a year-round landscape—to ask what a plant under consideration can do for you in the toughest months of the year, not just when it is in leaf or flower or when it puts on its fall foliage display.

The various white-skinned birches are not the only example, by any means. A recently promoted birch, the Heritage river birch (*Betula nigra* 'Heritage'), has better resistance to birch borer and other birch insect pests, and it features peeling bark of various pinkish white to salmon-tan shades.

A number of maples promise color and texture in the winter garden, including the paperbark maple (*Acer griseum*), which has cinnamon-colored bark that exfoliates, and the coralbark maple (*A. palmatum* 'Sango-kaku'), whose young wood is a brilliant coral color—startling against the winter sky. Unfortunately, the latter is not hardy for me, but moosewood (*A. pensylvanicum*), with its green trunk striped in white, is literally native—it makes up a main component of the woodland encircling my garden.

Among the shrubby twig dogwoods and willows, though, are plants to rival the coralbark maple's effect, if lower to ground level. The dogwoods (*Cornus* species), for instance, offer gold-, orange-, and red-stemmed possibilities, including *C. sericea* (yellow), *C. stolonifera* (yellow or red), and *C. sanguinea* 'Winter Beauty' (orange). From the willows you can have purple (*Salix purpurea*), yellow (various species), silvery white (*S. alba sericea*), or hot orange-red (*S. a.* 'Chermesina'). The color of the willow twigs will be most vibrant if they are stooled, or cut to the ground, in late winter each year, because it is the young wood that has the best color. With the dogwoods, cutting them back every third year (or cutting out one-third of the stems each year) produces the best color.

An enamel pan of paperwhite narcissus on the kitchen table, moving toward bloom.

FORCING BULBS

Three kinds of bulbs—paperwhite narcissus, amaryllis, and hyacinths—are so easy to force that there is no excuse not to try them (for amaryllis, see page 161). Hyacinth varieties labeled as suitable for forcing can simply be put in a special forcing glass filled with water to just below the base of the bulb—don't let it stand in the water; it will eventually awaken and push its roots down into the liquid for a drink.

Paperwhites can be forced in potting soil, or even in gravel, which is how I like to do it. In the bottom of any watertight pot or glass cylinder, place enough marbles, small stones, or gravel, or a mix of gravel and potting soil, to support the bulbs so that they have several inches for root growth down into the medium and are covered up to their waists or at most their shoulders in the stuff. Then water them (just enough so that the root area stands in water but not the bulb itself) and put them in a bright spot. Sometimes the foliage flops; that's why a tall glass cylinder works well, holding up the leaves while letting you still see their fresh color through the glass.

Keep hyacinth and paperwhite bulbs in the refrigerator until ready for use. Unlike amaryllis, they must be discarded after one use, since once forced they will not flower again.

Some bulbs need more in the way of a make-believe winter before they can be forced for indoor use ahead of their usual season. For this project, you'll need a cold frame or a cold, dark basement (38 to 45 degrees), or if you don't plan to have any food on hand for the next four months, you could use your refrigerator. (Some garden-crazy friends I know bought old refrigerators for their basements for this purpose. They plug them in only in the fall, for prechilling forced bulbs.)

You will need bulbs that are labeled as suitable for forcing, clean pots with drainage holes, and fresh potting soil. Grape hyacinths are a good choice, as are large-flowered crocuses, small daffodils, and certain tulips (with tulips, position the flat side of the bulb against the pot rim so the leaves will stretch up and over the rim later).

Plant between October 1 and the middle of November, depending on when you want the flowers to appear (which is somewhere around 18 weeks later, depending on the plant you work with). Layer some gravel in the bottom of the pots, and then add enough soil so that the tips of the bulbs set on top of the soil are about at the rim of the pot. There must be at least a couple of inches of soil beneath the bulbs to accommodate root development. Fill around the bulbs with more soil. Water well, label the pots with date and variety, and then place in a dark, cold spot for the number of chill weeks indicated for the plant, usually about 15. After the chill requirements have been fulfilled, bring the pots indoors into direct sunlight, water regularly, and expect blooms in several weeks.

BERRIED PLANTS

No fruiting plant in the garden outlasts the show put on by the deciduous hollies, with their heavy crops of glowing fruit that seem to linger until a flock of cedar waxwings comes to harvest them in late January or even February, as if they cannot resist the precious food one more minute. Berries like these that hang on the plant a long time are called persistent, and deciduous hollies such as native *Ilex verticillata* are certainly that.

I am also fond of *Aronia arbutifolia*, the chokeberry, another native American, and its close cousin *A. melanocarpa*. The former has glossy red fruit, the latter black, and both have about the hottest red foliage in fall of any plant around. I guess that makes up for the fact that the fruit is usually gone by sometime in December, as are the hips of even the longest-lasting rose, which by the time the frost has hit them again and again are finally ruined.

But the hollies make up for these other plants' lack of persistence. When growing hollies, whether deciduous ones or the better-known evergreens, the key to success is having the right pollinator on hand —a male plant that produces pollen but no fruit. Because the male plants of most species are not at all showy, some gardeners like to tuck them out of the way instead of in the main planting, which is fine. Lately, breeders have been introducing some dwarf males—heavy in pollen, but not so space-gobbling —a blessing in the small garden, where the space required for a boring-looking male might mean no hollies at all would be included.

The same pollinator will not work for every holly; the pollen-production phase of the two plants must coincide. Therefore it is very important to investigate what males you'll need and to install one nearby every cluster of females.

Besides being showy, and easy to grow, *I. verticillata* is happy in damp spots, just one more reason to love it, since little else is so accommodating.

RIGHT **A euphorbia, grown as a houseplant, makes shadow play on the bathroom curtain.** FOLLOWING PAGE **Pokeweed root in the snow.**

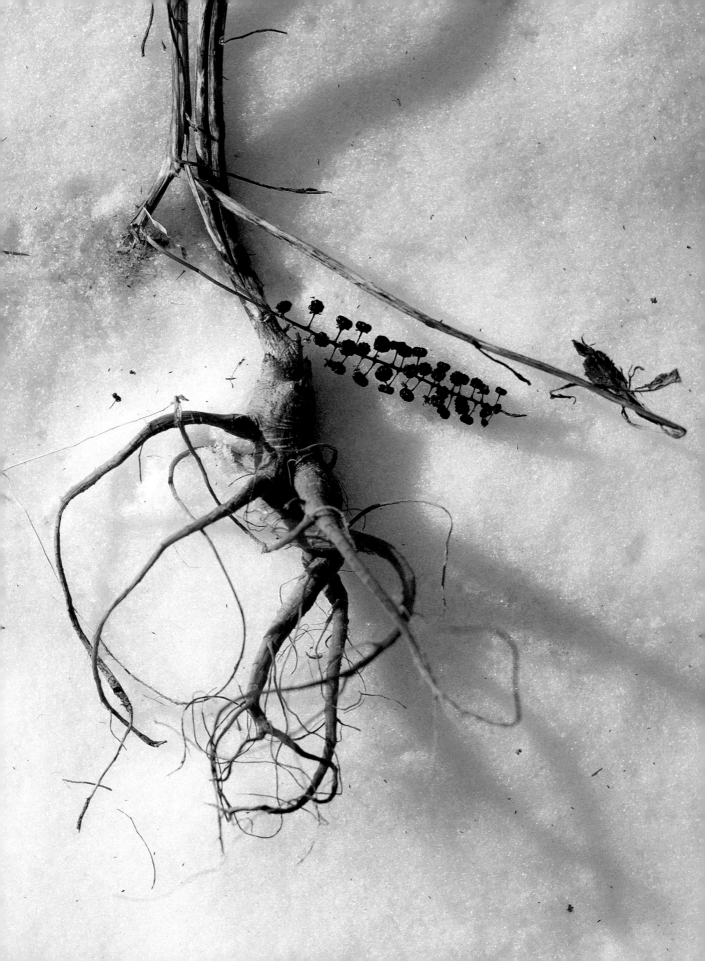

APPENDIX

And then there's all the rest of it—extra bits you're still wondering about. What follows is a compendium of details on topics from potatoes to houseplants, keeping critters out and the warmth in (with cloches). And, of course, you'll need to know how to combat those weeds.

A WINTER CUTTING GARDEN

To my eye, the cutting garden is the only place forsythia is always welcome. This otherwise weedy, often garish creature is a real pleasure when its stems are cut, brought indoors, and "forced" into bloom before their time (see "Forsythia Alternatives," page 62, for garden ideas for earliest spring). My old apple trees can always spare a few (zillion) branches, too, and pussy willows are their own special kind of preseason pleasure, not for sniffing as much as for petting.

Cherries, plums, peaches, shadbush (*Amelanchier* species), and Japanese quince are among the trees that can be easily forced, and don't overlook what I think may be the finest flowering tree of all for forcing, the maple. Maples are not thought of as having flowers, but they do, in wine reds and chartreuse.

A lot of fuss is made about hammering the ends of branches brought indoors for forcing, or slitting the stem ends lengthwise with a sharp knife, to increase conductivity of water. I have had success when I did this step, and also when I skipped it, and think it is more a matter of whether the branches are cut too early or brought into the indoor heat too fast that can hamper the success of forcing. I wait to cut branches until the flower buds have visibly swollen (meaning that the plant is within a couple of weeks of its normal outdoor bloom), and I first stand them in a bucket of water and set the bucket in the mudroom, where it is halfway between outdoor and indoor temperatures, for a couple of days, before arranging them in vases of water and moving them into the warmer house.

Many people lucky enough to possess a large specimen like to cut a branch of witch hazel (*Hamamelis* species; see page 41), but I am not so lucky to have enough wood to spare with this late-winter treasure.

Among the herbaceous plants, make room in the garden for "extras" of snowdrops, extra-early narcissus like 'February Gold', and other early bulbs, so that you can enjoy their beauty outdoors and indoors. Several dozen or more of each variety will surprise you when planted in an out-of-the-way spot or along the edges of your vegetable-garden beds. In shot glasses on the windowsill, with the late-winter light streaming through, these little creatures can ease the way to spring.

WILLING HOUSEPLANTS

If you have failed with houseplants, take a tip from the Victorians. I have had my best luck with indoor plants that have been out of favor for decades, such as the rhizomatous begonias and *Clivia miniata*, both of which were Victorian favorites and ought to be so prized again. Neither one asks more of me than a drink every week or so—and the clivia doesn't even ask for that from late fall through January, when I let it rest in a cool, bright room and go completely dry to induce its spikes of brilliant orange flowers. It will not bloom if watered year round, and it insists on a cool temperature while it rests. Fortunately, one of my unused bedrooms stays about 50 degrees all winter yet has bright, southern light.

In summer, the clivia goes outside to sit in the shade of a tree, where it gets good indirect light but no direct sun that would scorch its arching, leathery, dark green foliage. This unfussy creature doesn't even care to be repotted. It will let you know when to do so, by breaking right through the terra-cotta one day or in some such manner announcing its plans to move. Otherwise, leave it crowded.

My amaryllis, a collection of bulbs accumulated over the years, also spend the summer outdoors, in the vegetable garden, where they get lots of light but are similarly spared the direct, burning sun. Amaryllis bulbs like tight quarters and should be planted in pots that are only about an inch wider than the bulb all the way around (a 4-inch-diameter bulb would go in a 6-inch pot). The pots should be on the tall side, to accommodate the long and fleshy roots. About the time of frost, I bring the potted bulbs indoors and let them stand, unwatered, for a week or two, until their soil is fully dry, and then I stick them unceremoniously in the kitchen closet, where they will spend a couple of months in the dark, without a drink. Harsh, but necessary. By November, I haul them out and cut off their leaves, which by now should be looking sorry and yellow. I replenish the soil in the tops of the pots (if they've not been repotted for three years, I unpot them carefully, without startling the thick roots too much, and repot in all fresh soil). Then I stand them in a sink or rubber dishpan that is half full of water to soak up a long drink, set them in a bright window in a warm spot like the kitchen, and do nothing more. Some will wake up in a week or two, showing a hint of the tip of the fat flower bud I'm eager to see.

When those awakening pots feel dry, I water them again; the ones that still look asleep don't get any more water for a few weeks. If amaryllis aren't ready to awaken, heed their signals and let them rest awhile longer. Repeat the watering and waiting until you see life. Though I fertilize with a balanced formula all spring and summer, when the leaves are growing strongly, at this time of year I'm trying to coax flowers, not foliage, so if I feed at all it's with a formula with a high middle number (the P in the N-P-K ratio, which stands for phosphorus, the element that spurs root growth and flower production).

The only other things the amaryllis need to rebloom year after year are even simpler: Cut off the fading flowers, and then the flowering stem when it begins to shrivel, and foster as much strong green growth as you can all spring and summer. A stake may be required to hold up the flower stem on taller varieties, and even to support extra-long leaves so they don't snap. One more detail: Don't pitch a bulb that refuses to rebloom the first year after you have it in your care. Sometimes old habits, instilled when the bulbs were living at the nursery in Holland the year before, are hard to break.

Rhizomatous begonias need even less attention, and they reward the gardener with extravagantly shaped and colored foliage in shades of reds and greens and silvery touches. A plant may be only a few inches high and wide, or as big as a zucchini plant in early summer, depending on which variety you grow. Rhizomatous begonias like bright but indirect light,

occasional feeding, and regular watering, but only when they ask for it by looking a tiny bit droopy. Don't keep them soggy; let them go dry in between drinks, and watch for their signal of thirst. When the caterpillar-like rhizomes start to crawl out of the pots, many people think it's time to divide them into several smaller plants, but I prefer to pot the large-leaved kinds on to larger pots instead, for a giant octopus of a plant. If you want to keep them contained, use a razor blade to slice off a couple of inches of escaping rhizome, place it in a pot or tray with 2 inches of moist perlite and vermiculite, and keep it covered in a makeshift plastic tent (a see-through plastic storage box, like one used for shoes, is even better as a tiny propagating greenhouse). In a few weeks, the rhizome should have rooted in and will be ready for its own pot of a medium (use one formulated for ferns).

You can get all of these plants by mail, happily, from Logee's or Kartuz (see Sources).

PLANT "INCUBATORS"

The best broccoli I ever grew got its outdoor start under a tunnel of a spun-bonded synthetic fabric that I had never heard of before but saw in the back of a seed catalog. The product, called Reemay, was then more familiar to professional growers than to home gardeners; today it's commonplace, available at any garden center. I propped it up on a frame made of metal arches that I'd ordered along with the fabric, and the bugs were completely baffled.

Floating row covers, as such an arrangement is termed, are cozy season extenders (spring and fall, depending on the weight of the material) and bug stoppers (but open them up at pollination time for the insects you do want to reach your plants). I think every gardener who grows where the springs can be up-and-down affairs weather-wise should invest in some insurance in the form of protective devices, whether Reemay or individual hoods made of plastic or glass.

I have tried them all—fabrics, paper hotcaps, plastic gallon cartons with the bottoms cut off, even Wall O' Water plastic sleeves that you erect around stakes and then fill with water like a big, clear inflatable life jacket to collect and hold the earliest spring sunshine's warmth. I always have some individual caps of different sizes on hand to pop into place in case of a drop in temperature after the transplant date of tomatoes, eggplants, or peppers, and a bolt of Reemay is another essential you won't be sorry to have at the ready.

One more tool for the anticold arsenal is black plastic. Put it down several weeks before you plan to set out your tomatoes, peppers, eggplants, melons, pumpkins, and squash—any heat lovers that will appreciate the extra-toasty soil. I have left it in place all season some years, and simply made slits along the way to insert the seeds or plants, and it has worked fine. But it doesn't let a new supply of organic matter get next to the topsoil and decay, so it is better to lift it after a few weeks, at planting time. Roll and store it for next year.

POTATOES

Until I started growing them, I didn't know that the world of potatoes was anything more than simply baking, red, or new. For those who grow these easy vegetables, there can be spuds as small as your thumb (fingerling varieties such as 'Austrian Crescent' are great for salads and roasting) or as large as a pound-and-a-half meal ('Nooksack', a whopping russet-skinned type). They also come in many colors, both inside and out, including combinations of red, purple, and yellow. Lately, Yukon gold, with its creamy yellow flesh, has become a supermarket staple, and its success hints at how much better some potatoes are than the same old unnamed spuds.

Choose not just for size and color but also for texture, since potatoes may be mealy or smooth. It likewise makes sense to stagger the harvest by selecting some early varieties (65-plus days to harvest), midseason (85-plus days), and late (90-plus).

Potatoes go into the ground early, and according to the straight-and-narrow rules that means sometime a week or so before the final frost. In cooperative years, though, when the soil is workable and no longer sodden and cold, I like to jump the gun a couple of weeks further and get them in at the end of April.

Under ideal conditions, potatoes will yield about 14 pounds per pound of seed potatoes planted; I haven't achieved those results yet, but I keep trying and getting closer. They are planted in 6-inch-wide, 5-inch-deep trenches, leaving about a foot in the row between each seed potato (a smallish potato, or a wedge of a large potato that was cut to include some eyes, then allowed to cure a few days in the air before planting). As the foliage emerges and gets near a foot tall, I hill the plants up with extra soil. Here's where the work comes in. Where does the needed soil come from?

Since my soil is not rocky or too heavy, I sometimes dig a deeper trench to start with, leaving the loose excavated soil along each side of the trench. At hilling time, I just move it back onto the row of plants, never covering the foliage completely, but simply most of the way. When the plants grow up a bit again, I mulch them with a thick layer of oat straw.

An even easier method is to merely lay the seed potatoes on top of the soil in a row, a foot apart, then heap 6 to 8 inches of straw or hay mulch on top of them. Each time the shoots of the potato plants emerge, top-dress with more mulch; water regularly. Back-saving gardeners who use this method rave about the simplicity, and also about the clean potatoes they harvest, which were never underground. Potatoes are so eager to grow (as anyone who has kept a bag of them too long in the kitchen will confirm) that they can even be grown in a compost heap.

Whichever method you choose, do not give them lots of nitrogen (you'll get leaves, not tubers) or any lime, and be generous with the watering and sunshine. I leave my potatoes in the ground and use them from there as needed well into the fall, then dig the rest up carefully, working slowly so as not to pierce the tubers, and let them cure a bit in the last sunny days on the picnic table before putting them in bushel baskets in a spot where it is cool and dark, but not near freezing. A sampling of each variety can be carried over for next year's starts, so long as they are still firm and vital when the time comes to plant again.

ASPARAGUS

It should come as no surprise, since it's true so many other places: in the asparagus rows, males are in charge. 'Martha Washington' and 'Mary Washington' may be the names you've seen most often in asparagus lists in the catalogs, but they are the standard no more. Their weakness: The Washington strains include both male and female plants, and the males are far more productive if what you want is lots of spears.

In the mid-1980s, Rutgers University, a state institution in New Jersey, began a program to improve asparagus performance that focused on the extra productivity of the male plants. The resulting strains, most of which have the word *Jersey* in their names, are what you want to grow if you're going to go to the trouble of planting asparagus of your own. They waste no time or energy on seed production and go right to the task of making spears. They can be harvested more often (about every two to three days in a productive, established bed) and yield about 20 to 30 percent higher than the old varieties.

But asparagus tests even the most committed gardener, by asking for a major feat of excavation followed by a lot of patience. Whatever kind you're planting, you have to dig a trench about 18 inches wide and deep—no less than a foot in each direction, please. Since asparagus is best planted in spring, when dormant roots are sold by mail, prepare the bed the previous fall or in earliest spring. Order roots, or crowns, by mail for the freshest possible plants; they will be either one or two years old when you get them.

To prepare the bed, first test the soil pH by following the package instructions on a home test kit, like the one made by LaMotte and sold by Johnny's Selected Seeds (see Sources), or by taking a sample, according to their directions, to a local soil lab. The lab report will indicate how to amend the soil, and with what material, to suit your purpose; the typical routes are sulfur to acidify and lime to neutralize, but neither is a quick fix—or the whole answer. Adding large amounts of organic matter, preferably compost, to the soil should always be the first step; an organic soil is easier to pH-balance. For asparagus, you are aiming for a pH within the neutral range, or about 6.5 to 7.0.

As you dig, put the soil you excavate on a tarp or in wheelbarrows beside the site. Then layer into the bottom of the trench a few inches of well-rotted manure, sprinkle with rock phosphate and an all-natural organic fertilizer according to label directions, tamp the bottom, then fan the dormant asparagus roots out in the trench so they look like so many giant spiders. Space them about 18 inches apart within the row, and leave a few feet between parallel rows. When they are in place, backfill an inch or two of soil onto the plants and firm, then water. Once the crowns send up green shoots, shovel in another thin layer of soil (don't cover the tips completely), and repeat this step through the summer until the asparagus trench is filled back in. Keep the area weeded and watered.

Now comes the patience part. You cannot cut any spears until the third spring in the ground—a full two years after planting. Until then, simply let the plants go through their cycle of sprouting spears that turn ferny in summer. Don't cut off any foliage until cleanup of the bed in late winter or early spring.

The payoff is obvious, if you love asparagus. And, best of all, if kept weed-free and otherwise well-tended, an asparagus planting can last for up to 20 years.

SOWING FLOWERS IN THE FROST

A few annuals I am particularly fond of, including opium poppy and Flanders poppy (*Papaver somniferum* and *P. rhoeas,* respectively), larkspur (*Consolida ambigua*), and love-in-a-mist (*Nigella damascena*), seem to do best when they sow themselves and do not come easily from transplants. But if you do not have them in the first place, the chain reaction will not start.

When it is still quite cold, then when the ground is clear and soft enough to be scratched a bit, shallowly, with a cultivator, it's time to get out and sow these similarly tiny seeds. Simply press them into firm contact with the barely roughed-up soil surface. The trick is sowing thinly, but the extra time and care it takes is worth it, or you'll have to thin ruthlessly. The poppies will be up and growing soon (they look like tiny lettuce seedlings); the larkspur is more ferny. If all goes well, this is a one-time task, and then they'll be yours for years. It is also possible to sow these plants the previous fall, as they would sow themselves, and let the seeds overwinter and get off to a quick start. I find that I can barely get an inch of clear soil then, though, because I have not completely cleaned up yet, and also if I have forgotten to order them, there are no seeds to be had locally. Either way will work, so long as the plants get a dose of cold before they are meant to germinate.

MULCH

"God invented mulching," wrote Ruth Stout, whose offbeat 1961 classic *Gardening Without Work* promised freedom from weeds and optimum soil health to gardeners who piled on 8 inches of hay mulch, and not a blade less. (Stout's ideas have been repackaged by Rodale in *Ruth Stout's No-Work Garden Book,* which is easier to locate than the original book.) Her somewhat unconventional tradition, more the stuff of homesteaders than backyard types, is mulching at its maximum mass; the gardener simply pulls away a bit to make an opening for planting seeds or seedlings. No tilling required. Though perfectly acceptable in the vegetable garden, the hay-pile look is generally out of place in the front yard or the perennial border. But Stout was definitely on to something.

Mulch serves many important purposes and can be made from many materials. Using the wrong kind, or even the right one but at the wrong time, can completely defeat the purpose of mulching.

Mulches can suppress weeds; help slow evaporation of moisture; keep root zones of plants cool; foster abundant life in the soil in the form of organisms from microbes to earthworms; improve soil texture over time, and also add organic matter to it as the mulch slowly breaks down; reduce compaction of the underlying soil (raindrops, not just footsteps, are surprisingly big culprits, pounding the soil relentlessly; the mulch mitigates the impact).

The biggest mistakes are mulching too early in summer, before the soil has a chance to warm; leaving a wintertime mulch on too late in the spring; or mulching too deeply (unless you are trying the Stout thing). Piling 6 or 8 or 10 inches of supersize wood chips right up against the trunks of trees and shrubs is wasteful and unattractive, and it can even promote disease and prevent rain from penetrating to the roots; $1\,^1/_2$ to 3 inches is plenty.

Never mulch when you do your garden cleanup in spring; things have barely come alive, and the soil is usually damp and cold. Mulching will keep the cold in the ground. Wait until things are really growing strongly—for me mulching time is sometime in June.

The best mulches of all are organic in nature, meaning they are made of formerly living material that will gradually degrade and add to the soil. Fine-textured ones are particularly suited to decomposition and will have to be replenished slightly each year to make up for losses returned to the earth. Finely textured bark (shredded or the so-called mininuggets) is a popular mulch, but never use the big, baked-potato-size wood chips in the garden—they look unnatural and take years to break down. I like partially composted, shredded leaves as a mulch, or better yet aged (composted) stable bedding—manure-enhanced wood shavings. Expensive fine-textured choices include cocoa hulls (for a peculiar, chocolate-smelling yard) and buckwheat hulls.

Oat straw is one of my favorite mulches for the rougher look of the vegetable garden, but I don't use it on my flower beds. I don't use hay anywhere. Though it is less expensive than oat straw, it is much weedier and sows its grassy progeny all over the garden. In 8-inch layers as Ruth Stout recommended, there would no doubt be fewer weeds, however.

The common recommendation is to add nitrogen fertilizer to areas where wood-based mulches such as chips, sawdust, and wood shavings are being applied, to offset leaching of nitrogen from the soil, which woody materials use when they break down. Instead, pile these materials up for a year or more and compost them before using them as mulch. As for sawdust, don't use the kind that's generated by sanding and cutting wood for carpentry at home; it's too fine-textured, and it turns into a sodden mass. Mills may have something closer to wood shavings, which are okay and are the stuff often used in animal stalls.

Wintertime mulch is another case altogether and is usually applied too early. The idea isn't to insulate plants from the cold, it's to keep the roots and surrounding soil frozen in place so they won't heave and thaw in ups and downs of winter weather. In areas where the ground freezes, pile on the mulch only after the plants are really dormant, after the first hard freeze.

For topping a pathway, you can use the mulch that best suits your aesthetic sense. Shredded bark works well in a woodland area, for instance, and gravel is effective near the beach. Underline the path with permeable landscape fabric, not sheets of plastic, so that water can drain through while weeds are being suppressed. Thick layers of newsprint can also be used to line a path under another mulch, although it will not retain its weed-suppressing capacity.

If you don't mind the way it looks, black plastic sold in rolls at nurseries and through the mail can be used as a mulch material, but because it heats up the soil its use should be reserved for crops that can handle that extra heat: tomatoes, peppers, pumpkins, melons, salvias, zinnias. Cut large X's in the plastic and fold it back to insert seeds once the soil has warmed below it (a few weeks after you lay the plastic down), or tuck plants into the openings. Pull up the plastic from year to year to give the soil a chance to breathe and drain.

FERTILIZERS

Bagged fertilizers, whether chemical ones or their all-natural, organic counterparts, are no substitute for building healthy soil (see "Soil Preparation," page 53). Though I firmly believe in purchasing only the latter, which are made from renewable resources such as waste products and by-products of other industries, I use them as supplements, the way I use multivitamins for myself. I still eat three squares a day, and the soil needs real food, too, not just a booster here and there.

The numbers on a fertilizer bag are the so-called N-P-K ratio, the percent of nitrogen, phosphorus, and potash (or potassium, chemical symbol K) inside the bag. Simply speaking, nitrogen is for green growth; phosphorus is for roots, flowers, and fruit; potash is for general vigor and disease resistance. A so-called balanced fertilizer, often recommended in books, is one that has equal percentages of each element.

With chemical fertilizers, the numbers are much higher than with organic formulations. A standard is 10-10-10 or 5-10-5, meaning there are those percentages of each element in the bag (the rest is filler). You won't find those totals in any organic formulation. In fact, if the total of the three numbers on a so-called organic or natural bag adds up to more than 15, I'm suspicious. Unless blood meal—an organic material very high in nitrogen—is in the ingredient list, I suspect that the formula has a chemical booster in it.

Labels can be confusing, since many companies have put flowers and butterflies on their bags but still have chemicals inside. Learn to read what's inside; the more plain-English words you see on the ingredient list, the better. Typical nonchemical ingredients are dried animal wastes, rock dusts, bonemeal, alfalfa meal and other meals, and dried blood.

All-natural, organic fertilizers aren't a quick solution, since most of them break down slowly (blood meal is a notable exception). Even chemical fertilizers aren't instant remedies, except the so-called soluble ones, like all those blue powders and liquids millions of people dilute to pour on their houseplants and garden plants every day, which deliver nutrients faster than do granular formulas. For a natural liquid fertilizer, I use concentrated liquid seaweed and fish emulsion, diluted according to the label directions.

Although compost is not strictly speaking a fertilizer, I recommend it highly as a soil conditioner. Depending on the source, compost does have a degree of fertility (aged animal manures tend to have more than, say, rotted leaves), but most of all what it does is to lend the soil a capacity to handle nutrients and moisture more effectively and make them available to plants. Pile it on, as much as you can produce or acquire—or at least until your back aches too much each spring and fall to toss another shovelful around.

ANIMALS, GOOD AND BAD

Do tomato hornworms come in the seed packet with the tomatoes? Do Mexican bean beetles hibernate inside the bean seeds? And how do woodchucks always seem to know the grass (or tulips, roses, lettuce, sedum . . . you name it) is greener on the other side of the fence, meaning in my yard?

There are limits to what can be done about animals in the garden, since if I were to try to get the edge over every kind, I'd spend all my time on fauna and none on flora. I focus my attentions on those that simply cannot coexist with a successful garden, including deer, woodchucks (also called groundhogs), and rabbits. If you have a problem with any of them, particularly the first two, I think you will agree. They are far too destructive to be allowed to have their fill.

They clearly must be kept out, which means serious measures. I have tried spraying commercial repellents, sprinkling blood meal around, spreading the commercial fertilizer called Milorganite (made from sewage sludge and completely inoffensive to humans but anathema to deer), bars of soap and sachets of soap shavings, aluminum pie plates on strings hanging in the wind, and even—yes, I admit it—expensive, store-bought coyote urine. But I do not have time to respray every inch of my plantings every time heavy rain rinses the garden clean or to replenish the other materials, which are all fairly expensive. Besides, I'm not convinced they are 100 percent effective.

Fence them out, period. My two vegetable gardens are fenced against the rabbits and chucks, who don't climb but will occasionally try to burrow under. For this reason, the vegetable-fence wire mesh must be buried a foot underground. If you have these large pests, they'll simply relocate to your flowers and shrubs if you put your food crops out of reach, and so on. They have to be removed, which means different things to different people and in different areas. I recommend consulting the Yellow Pages for a licensed trapper, unless you are confident about taking matters into your own hands. Either way, be sure you are operating within the letter of local law.

Live traps, such as Haveaharts, will catch small animals successfully, but think in advance what you will do with an agitated woodchuck or a frightened rabbit (the possibilities do not include relocating it to the yard of an unpleasant neighbor or the local park).

For deer, fencing the entire property or the main

zone to be landscaped is really the only answer, and after long research and hours of cost comparisons, I decided on a heavy, black polypropylene mesh fence that measures about 7 feet high. I had wanted to use seven-strand high-tensile electric wire, but for a couple of acres in my rural area, where prices are admittedly very low, with posts and power pack that would run more than $5,000, installed professionally. The poly netting can be attached (by the homeowner, as I've done) to a perimeter of trees, which substantially reduces the number of posts needed and it also requires almost no maintenance, lasts 10 years, and is invisible from about 20 feet. There is no current to get interrupted by a falling branch or heavy load of weeds or snow along the ground. In all, it cost less than half the estimates for electric and less than any kind of wire mesh would have run (even finding a kind of wire that is 7 feet high is a challenge). A friend combined a couple of tiers of chicken wire held up with baling wire to trees along her woodland edge; the rest of her property is enclosed by a high board fence. Another used tall concrete reinforcing wire.

Since deer, like rodents and rabbits, will try to get under or through a fence they can't get over, evaluate possible materials with this in mind. My mesh is pinned to the ground with U-shaped wire staples.

On my front perimeter, I chose an ornamental kind of fence—traditional 4-foot wooden pickets—but I attached them to 4 x 4 posts that are about 8 feet out of the ground and capped decoratively on top. The reason for the high posts is to continue the barrier without erecting a high board fence out front (illegal in many communities, and also costly, and anything but welcoming aesthetically). From post to post above the pickets, I strung two strands of taut fencing wire, as if I were making an electric fence, about 18 inches apart. My goal all the way around was to have a 7-foot barrier. Deer can probably jump higher, but there's a limit to what I can do to keep them out if they really want to fly.

To train the deer to avoid the fence, it's critical to tie white streamers about a foot long on the new mesh fence (plastic or wire mesh) at least every 10 feet (which I also did on the strands of wire I used out front). Otherwise they will walk right into it and get startled or even hurt. After a few months, you can remove the streamers (hopefully by then they will have found another path through the area).

For a smaller property, try a trick I once saw in

California: two parallel, 4-foot fences, spaced about 5 feet apart. The same way that a small, fenced enclosure like a vegetable garden looks uninviting to deer, so does the double row of fence. Not wanting to land inside a tight space, they walk around it. Yet the view is uninterrupted by high fencing—a good compromise, but expensive for a large area.

Just as I focus on the worst of the animals, leaving the squirrels and chipmunks and such to root around with impunity, when it comes to bugs I concentrate only on the ones that cannot be tolerated. Japanese beetles, for instance, awaken in my region every Fourth of July and quickly skeletonize the foliage of roses, raspberries, beans, and many other plants I grow. While I am not alarmed about a leaf munched here and there, Japanese beetles are another matter. Trapping them with beetle bags scented with a phony sexual lure works somewhat, but it is reported to attract extra beetles from nearby plots unless everybody's doing it around your neighborhood. The only reasonably good solution, then, is a slow-acting one: to infect the turf, under which the beetle grubs hibernate, with milky spore disease, a safe product for us and for the environment that over a couple of years builds up enough punch to kill the grubs. It is available as a powder at any garden center.

Various beetles, such as squash beetles, Mexican bean beetles, and Colorado potato beetles, are dangerous because they spread fatal plant diseases such as wilt while they gnaw your plants. Floating row covers are the best line of defense. With the potatoes, a thick straw mulch layer also seems to deter them. Squash vine borers can kill melons, pumpkins, cukes, and squash; tunnels of the fabric suspended over wire hoops will help thwart them, too, as will mounding soil over the base of the plants once they are established, since these insects almost always do their damage in the bottom 6 inches or so of the main stem.

Outsmart bugs as much as possible with the timing of your crops. The local Cooperative Extension Service in my county, part of a statewide network that helps farmers and gardeners, has information about insect arrivals. If I pay attention, I can do a lot better than if I play right into the bugs' hands (mouths) and have succulent plants ready the day they arrive.

Diatomaceous earth—not the kind used in pool filters but the product specifically rated for agricultural/horticultural use—is anathema to soft-bodied pests like slugs, because it is actually many very sharp particles, and it can be applied as a dust over the soil surface. Always wear a mask when using this product, which like any dust can irritate the lungs, and follow package directions for application rates.

When I do experience a bad-bug population buildup, I roughly turn the soil during one of the late-winter thaws, just as another freeze is about to set in. It's amazing who is sleeping underneath (and gets caught without their blanket and frozen to death).

ROSES THAT REPEAT

There are so many classes of roses—hybrid teas and old-fashioned shrubs, ramblers and climbers and so forth—that it is sometimes hard to keep them all straight. Most important of all when choosing a rose, however, is knowing whether it's a one-time bloomer (nonremontant) or a repeater (remontant).

To figure that out, you will either have to look it up in a rose book or, if the plant is big enough to show signs of last year's or this year's bloom, examine it to see where it makes its flowers. The ones that bloom only once a year (in June in my area) bloom on old wood—canes that matured the previous year—which thereby limits them to a single performance. Roses whose flowers are borne on fresh new growth from the current season can keep on growing new wood on which to form blossoms over a long period. Those are the repeaters. (Of course, if it's August or October and the rose is blooming, you'll know it is a repeater.)

The best of these everblooming roses continue through the season, and they are the ones to look for if you are considering the rose for a prominent location, since they won't peter out and leave a big gap after a mere couple of weeks of glory. Generally speaking, everbloomers make the most satisfying choice, especially for beginning gardeners, though I have made room for a few shrubby old-fashioned garden roses just for the special quality they bring to the garden in June, even though they do not repeat.

Certain classes of roses, such as ramblers, are always one-time bloomers; climbers, on the other hand, have the ability to rebloom. One factor that helps ensure this (and better bloom in general on all roses, even one-timers) is how horizontally the canes are placed by the gardener, since roses don't have holdfasts, tendrils, or other means of attaching themselves to a pergola, wall, or arbor. The more horizontally you position the branches when you tie them up, the better; the roses respond favorably through some internal mechanism to this extra help.

There is one rose I consider a must-have, no matter how fleeting its moment of bloom. *Rosa rubrifolia* (more recently listed as *R. glauca*), with its leaves a blue-green tinged with wine and olive, is exceptional all season. Its small, single, clear pink flowers are nice, too, but short-lived, but then come the large, reddish hips. Between the flowers, fruit, and foliage, no rose does more for a mixed border than this one.

Although the concept of a rose garden—an exclusive habitat for roses only, or just about—is a classic fantasy, roses are more successful (particularly in a small home-garden setting) if integrated rather than segregated. They fit nicely into the flower garden or the sunny shrub border and are enchanting clambering over the vegetable-garden fence or up the sunny side of a building. The new landscape or carpet types can be used to hold a bank or for another ground-cover task. If you want a roses-only area anyhow, plan to underplant it or edge it with a flowering ground cover like catmint (*Nepeta mussinii*) or lady's mantle (*Alchemilla mollis*) or even annual sweet alyssum (sow the seeds in earliest spring; if left to go to seed, they will usually return next year). They'll help knit the roses together as well as clothe their ankles in a flattering manner.

WATERING METHODS

I try to water as little as possible, both because it takes so much time and because I do not want to be irresponsible with this most precious resource. When I do water, I choose my method carefully, for each plant.

My first line of defense against having to water all the time is proper soil preparation (see "Soil Preparation," chapter 2), adding lots of organic material that will help the soil hold and conduct water. My second tactic is to mulch, preventing evaporation as well as shading and cooling roots. I use a fine-textured organic material such as finely shredded bark (on paths and in woodsy areas), composted stable bedding made of wood shavings (in flower borders), and oat straw (in vegetable beds).

Obviously, though, a gardener will need to water sometimes. I judge the need first by the weather: if an inch of moisture has accumulated in the plastic rain gauges around the yard that week, I feel less panicky. It is not all rainfall numbers that make the difference on how plants fare; after high winds, very high temperatures, or other stressors, an inch of rain may not suffice. Besides reading the gauges, I look for visual clues, and I stick my fingers into the ground here and there to see what's happening down below.

I do not fight the lawn's desire to go brown in a hot, dry August; it will green up again when the heat subsides and rains resume. I use my water instead for the plants that will not live or, in the case of food-bearing ones, will not produce a crop. Raspberries, for instance, will not bear much of anything in a dry year; tomatoes are stingy, too. I also cater to the youngest plants (new transplants) and the oldest (aging trees) most of all.

The timing and method of applying water are critical, since a couple of inches of water sprayed into the air at high noon on a hot, sunny day will not amount to as much as half that placed right at the root zone in the morning. Generally the rule is to get it right to the root zone without losses to evapotranspiration.

Getting to the root zone does not mean letting a hose run on the ground at the base of a tree trunk all day or night, or spraying the surface of your whole garden from a handheld hose-end sprayer for 10 minutes. Know what the extent of a plant's root zone is: how wide it is and how deep. With a large tree, for instance, it is pointless to water the trunk. Starting a foot and a half out from it, spiral a series of connected perforated hoses (also called soaker hoses) to a foot or two beyond the dripline (the perimeter of the tree formed by the reach of its branches). Water slowly all night long; for old trees, in a very dry spell repeat every week.

In most cases, the watering method preferred for ease, cost effectiveness, and water conservation is drip irrigation. I could write a book about this topic, but here are the basics: the current state-of-the-art drip systems (such as the one using components by Netafim, a company all the experts highly rate and which professional installers rely on) can be installed as a do-it-yourself project, once the vendor helps you determine what parts you need and the configuration.

Drip systems are inexpensive, and they do not require trenching or burying (placing the lines on the soil surface, or just below the mulch for aesthetic reasons, is fine). In areas that need to be tilled regularly, such as a vegetable garden, the harness of tubing and fittings for each bed can simply be unplugged or lifted out of place and then later returned to their positions.

It was formerly recommended that emitters (the holes or valves where the water comes out) be positioned near every plant, but that's no longer the thinking. Instead, the idea is to soak the soil around an area, so it's less tricky than calculating every inch of your garden layout and where every plant is.

Don't buy kits in the garden center; go with the materials the professionals use, such as the ones sold by The Natural Gardening Company and The Urban Farmer Store (see Sources). They will help you map out a system for your place alone; a kit can't.

Whatever system you use, do not leave it on a timer once installed and forget about it. Tuesdays at 7 A.M. and Thursdays at 8—or whatever preprogrammed settings you chose—may not always be right for watering, week in and week out. Watering systems—from handheld hoses and cans to fancy in-ground sprinklers and drip-irrigation setups—need human judgment to make them perform best.

As low-tech and old-fashioned as they seem, I would not be without a couple of different sprinklers, which continue to be important tools for special garden applications. When I have recently seeded an area of the lawn, for instance, a sprinkler is the right watering tool. I also use them to water my crack-and-crevice gardens, such as the front walk and patio.

THE REALITY OF WEEDS

Alice B. Toklas once asked Gertrude Stein what she saw when she closed her eyes. *"Weeds,"* Stein replied.

It must have been summer, when despite the gardener's best effort, weeds seem to grow a foot a week, outpacing the garden's desired residents.

Whether in summer, earliest spring, or latest fall, weeds must be tackled as they occur. The best time by far to weed is after a rainstorm; don't miss this natural opportunity. I do not use chemical herbicides—weed killers—in my garden and have resorted to them only twice in 10 years, both times to check a particularly aggressive stand of poison ivy.

Even with poison ivy, however, I am more inclined to pull it out than to spray it, though this involves very careful concentration and should never be done by anyone who has had a bad allergic reaction to the plant. Wearing disposable surgical latex gloves, a long-sleeved shirt, and long pants tucked into rubber boots, work not just to remove the foliage but to uncover the root system and remove it. Note that all parts of the plant are poisonous—roots and all, whether dormant or in midsummer's leafy glory.

Put the poison ivy you dig up into a plastic garbage bag as you go (being careful not to contaminate the outside of the bag); never burn it, since the fumes can cause a very serious reaction in the lungs. Tie the bag closed and put it promptly in the trash. Do not touch your face or hair or any other exposed part while working, and once finished, immediately peel down and deposit the clothes in the washer, then remove and bag the gloves in plastic and throw them away, too. I keep a bottle of Tecnu brand soap on hand, with which I wash my hands and arms according to the label directions, as a further preventive step, and then I shower.

One more tip: Remember that the boots and any tools you used are probably full of ivy oil, too, from which you can get a rash. To be safe, you may wish to scrub them before removing your gloves.

The first step toward managing your weeds is to get to know them: identify your real troublemakers, and find out how best to tackle them. By no means allow them to flower and set seed. Deep-rooted weeds are particularly challenging, since even a bit of flesh left underground will usually mean more plants next year. A fishtail weeder—that inexpensive tool with a wooden or plastic handle and a small, notched M-shaped blade on a long neck—can be invaluable. In tight spaces, such as the cracks in the sidewalk and patio, where weeds love to nest, try a butter knife.

Although it is a disputed practice, I compost my weeds, except for seed-laden ones, which I throw out. Bulbous ones, like onion grass, or insidious runners, like witchgrass, may also be better discarded, unless you know your compost pile's temperature and are also willing to let things cook for a long time. I do not use my compost right away, and the pile generates a lot of heat, so the weeds and their seeds get cooked for a year or longer before I return them to the garden, hopefully rendered benign. In a cooler compost pile, I would not advise incorporating pesky weeds.

Sometimes there are so many weeds that you will never get the upper hand. With a new garden area, in particular, often it's worth waiting a season or two before planting, to be rid of the weeds. The best method for killing them safely without chemicals is called solarization, which means cooking them to death with the help of the sun and a layer of plastic. First clean up the area a bit to remove really large plants, then lay the plastic over the weeds and infested soil, weighted down with stones or timbers so that it will stay in place securely for a whole spring and summer at the very least—until next spring is better. The plastic (black works best) collects the sun's heat and that helps to kill not just the aboveground foliage but also many of the seeds lurking in the soil. Solarization is obviously less efficient in shady areas than in sunny ones, but where it works, it can even be used instead of herbicide to kill off an old, ratty-looking lawn that needs replacing; once the grass is dead, till the soil, rake out the clods of old turf and compost them, and prepare the seedbed for replanting.

REAL-LOOKING LILIES

I am not one to spout religion, or even to practice it. But in the case of lilies, I will have to say this: the ones made by whoever is responsible for the creation of things are much better than the ones made by mere humans. Stay away from unnatural-looking, stiff, upward-facing lilies in favor of those that flare outward like trumpets or dangle like bells.

The species lilies—that is, ones that have not been hybridized—are naturally graceful, and many are exceedingly fragrant. *Lilium henryi*, with its orange flowers and sweet scent, is one possibility. *L. regale* has extra-large white trumpets that are stained purple-pink on the outsides. Native *L. superbum*, the Turk's-cap lily, is a species that can tolerate moderately wet soil, a condition under which bulbous plants normally rot.

L. martagon is especially beautiful, with its many smallish pink or maroon or white flowers. One of the most striking uses of a lily I have ever seen was a stand of martagons at Powis Castle in Wales, in the light shade of an open woodland, where dozens of stems stood up amidst a stand of ferns. This brings up the point of where to site lilies, which is usually in full sun, although the martagons do adapt to light shade.

L. auratum, which has white petals banded yellow down the center, is another beauty. One favorite of all lilies is the Madonna lily (*L. candidum*), the oldest lily in cultivation, and as its name suggests it is the purest white (and also highly fragrant). Most lilies are planted in fall, as soon as they arrive from the dealer, or they can be installed in spring. This last one, however, asks for extra-early attention. Get it in the ground in early September, so it has time to make a tuft of greenery aboveground before winter sets in.

BASIC BOTANICAL LATIN confounds beginning gardeners. The worst part: worries about proper pronunciation. I only wish that someone had told me twenty years ago that any pronunciation was

fine—and light-years better than imprecise common names. Botanical Latin, it turns out, isn't a real language at all—it's not the tongue of ancient Rome—but a system of nomenclature (or naming) invented by Carl von Linne in 1753.

How do you pronounce the words of a language that doesn't belong to any one nation or people, exactly? Any way you like. What's important is that you learn the words and let them help you to find the plant you really want. As a bonus, certain botanical Latin words used to name various plants often also reveal that plant's characteristics. This is particularly true among the species names, or "specific epithets," the second word in each two-part botanical name, which modifies the first word, the genus name. What follows is a sampling, in each case expressed in the *-us* ending (*-a* and *-um* are also used when the gender of the subject being modified is appropriate):

COLOR

Yellow may be expressed with *flavus* (a pale version), *luteus,* and *citrinus* (lemon-colored).

Red is *rubus;* rosy-pink is *roseus.*

Purple is simple: just say *purpureus.* If it's very dark, it might be *atropurpureus.*

White is *albus;* black is *nigrum.*

Silver is expressed as *argenteus;* gold as *aureus.*

As for good old green, when it's noted it might be *viridis* (or *sempervirens* in the case of evergreen).

There are various words for blue, including *azureus* (a sky-blue color) and *caeruleus* (somewhat darker).

Variegated leaves or flowers are sometimes labeled *variegatus,* but might also be called *pictus* (which means painted, and is used to indicate bright coloration of other kinds, too).

GROWTH HABIT

If a plant is graceful or slender, it might be designated *gracilis.* If it is globe-shaped, *globosus* might be more appropriate. A pyramid, not surprisingly, is often expressed by *pyramidalis.*

A shrubby plant might be labeled *fruticosus* or *frutescens.* Upright and columnar? Look for the words *fastigiatus* or *columnaris.* Downright narrow, with nearly parallel sides: *linearis.*

A dwarf plant might be *nanus* or *pumilus;* a creeping one, *repens;* one flat on the ground, *prostratus* or *procumbens.* If they spread in a straggly manner, the specific epithet *divaricatus* is a possibility. If instead the plant climbs, it could be called *scandens.*

SURFACE TEXTURE OR PATTERN

Pleated leaves might be indicated by the word *plicatus.* Woolly ones are often labeled *lanatus.*

Mollis means soft (because the plant is covered with soft hairs); *glaucus* plants are coated in what's called bloom (a fine white powdery coating).

If the surface glistens, it could be called *fulgens.* If it's spiny, *spinosus* is a more appropriate epithet.

Spots might be indicated by the word *punctatus.*

FRAGRANCE

Inodorus means a plant doesn't have a fragrance. *Aromaticus* and *fragrans* mean that it does. But so do *pungens* (pungent), *odoratus* (sweet-smelling), and *foetidus* (fetid, or stinking).

BLOOM TIMES

Some epithets, such as *praecox,* mean simply early. Spring interest is expressed by *vernalis;* summer by *aestivalis;* fall by *autumnalis,* and winter by *hyemalis.*

HABITAT OF ORIGIN

Plants from wet places are often called *palustris* (or *aquaticus,* if they actually live in water). Those from rocky areas may bear the specific epithet *saxatilis;* if sand was in their background, *arenarius* is the word. Woodland denizens may be *sylvaticus* or *sylvestris;* those from above the treeline are *alpinus.*

SOURCES

The boom in mail-order gardening, combined with the advent of really fast shipping nationwide, means you can get virtually anything anywhere anytime. But how to handle the delivery when it arrives?

I had grown accustomed to the small miracle of plants in pots buffered with wads of newspaper actually making it through days in the mail. Others came in partitioned corrugated boxes with a cell per plant, like liquor does (a wasteful form of packing, but also very secure). Lately, however, it seems as though shippers have been turning to the kitchen, not the mailroom, for their ideas on packing materials. Plants are starting to show up without pots at all, their root balls swaddled in aluminum foil or, more commonly, plastic wrap. In the case of one misguided shipper recently, I even received herb plants that were packed in real popped popcorn—not a pretty sight.

With any mail-order arrival, the key is to get it out into the fresh air fast (not the wind and direct sun, though). There the plant can stretch out and feel normal again, the way that people do after a long plane ride cramped in a tiny seat. This is a little trickier with the potless specimens, since you can't just line them up outside in the shade and water them until you're good and ready to plant them. Their root balls will fall apart if you remove the foil or plastic; if you don't, they will cook in the heat or suffocate (this is particularly true with the plastic). I find this all a little off-putting, and aside from the important issue of wasted plastic and garbage accumulation, I long for all those pots again. I'd be willing to pay a deposit for every pot and mail them back for credit, though I don't suppose that would be a popular solution.

The most vulnerable plants of all are those that come bare-root—that is, not only without a pot but also without soil. This is a standard method for shipping roses, fruit trees and bushes, and many other woody plants, as well as herbaceous plants that grow from fleshy roots, rhizomes, or crowns such as strawberry, asparagus, ferns, and lily-of-the-valley. Don't be afraid of bare-root; it's the best way to ship things without adding greatly to the cost. The perennials you purchase at the garden center in May were probably delivered bare-root two months earlier, then potted up in greenhouses to get them going.

At home, time bare-root plants to arrive early, too, although not until it is possible to work the soil (and late enough that they won't freeze solid in shipping). If you are able to hold them in their sleepy state of semidormancy for a week or two or three, then they can come even earlier. A refrigerator will work, if you can spare the room, and so will a mudroom or garage where the temperature hovers from the mid-30s to the mid-40s.

Soak woody bare-root plants in a deep bucket of water overnight before planting day, to help invigorate them. And with any transplant, give it extra care the first days and weeks outdoors—water regularly as the soil dries until the plants root in.

SEEDS

BOUNTIFUL GARDENS 18001 Shafer Ranch Road, Willits, CA 95490; (707) 459-6410; catalog free. Openpollinated, untreated seeds, primarily of vegetables and cover crops, aimed at organic gardeners.

THE COOK'S GARDEN P.O. Box 335, Londonderry, VT 05148-0535; (802) 824-3400; as the name sounds, a kitchen gardener's essential list, plus flowers.

THE FLOWERY BRANCH P.O. Box 1330, Flowery Branch, GA 30542; (405) 536-8380; catalog $2. Herbs and everlastings, including many unusual ones.

THE FRAGRANT PATH P.O. Box 328, Fort Calhoun, NE 68028; no phone; catalog $1. A charming mix of (mostly) fragrant things, including a great selection of annual vines.

GARDEN CITY SEEDS 778 Highway 93 North, Room 13, Hamilton, MT 59840; (406) 961-4837; catalog free. Seeds for a wide range of vegetable and some ornamentals, geared to cold climates and short seasons.

J.L. HUDSON, SEEDSMAN P.O. Box 1058, Redwood City, CA 94064; no telephone; catalog $1 in postage stamps. Quirky and diverse, from vegetable and flower seeds to ones for growing rare trees, including seeds of Mexican Indian crops.

JOHNNY'S SELECTED SEEDS Foss Hill Road, Albion, ME 04910; (207) 437-4301; catalog free. Every seed you'll need for the garden (especially a short-season one), plus a fine range of supplies and tools.

NICHOLS GARDEN NURSERY 1190 North Pacific Highway, Albany, OR 97321-4580; (503) 928-9280; catalog free. Seeds (and some plants) for herbs, vegetables, and flowers, with a homey touch.

SELECT SEEDS ANTIQUE FLOWERS 180 Stickney Hill Road, Union, CT 06076-4617; (203) 684-9310; catalog $1. Charming, old-fashioned varieties of perennial and annual flowers, including many annual vines.

SHEPHERD'S GARDEN SEEDS 30 Irene Street, Torrington, CT 06790; (203) 482-3638; catalog free. Seeds for a beautiful and delicious kitchen garden, and many flowers.

SOUTHERN EXPOSURE SEED EXCHANGE P.O. Box 170, Earlysville, VA 22936; (804) 973-4703; catalog $2. Modern and old-fashioned vegetables and some flowers, including many heat-tolerant kinds.

TOMATO GROWERS SUPPLY COMPANY P.O. Box 2237, Fort Myers, FL 33902; (813) 768-1119; catalog free. Several hundred kinds of tomatoes, plus about 100 peppers.

PLANTS

ARBORVILLAGE P.O. Box 227, Holt, MO 64048; (816) 264-3911; catalog $1. Trees and shrubs, including many that are hard to find.

B&D LILIES 330 P Street, Port Townsend, WA 98368; (206) 385-1738; catalog $3. As the name suggests, lilies, lilies, and more lilies.

CANYON CREEK 3527 Dry Creek Road, Oroville, CA 95965; (916) 533-2166; catalog $2. Choice perennials (some, like salvias, to use as annuals in colder zones), including many unusual things.

COMPANION PLANTS 7247 N. Coolville Ridge Road, Athens, OH 45701; (614) 592-4643; catalog $2. An exhaustive list of herbs (plants, too).

THE DAFFODIL MART Route 3, Box 794, Gloucester, VA 23061; (804) 693-3966; catalog free; every manner of daffodil, and every other bulb you could want as well.

FORESTFARM 990 Tetherow Road, Williams, OR 97544; (503) 846-7269; catalog $3. A giant list of woody plants and herbaceous ones, available in small sizes

(or large if you want to fork over the shipping costs).

GOSSLER FARMS NURSERY 1200 Weaver Road, Springfield, OR 97478-99691; (503) 746-3922; catalog $2. Fine woody plants, including many magnolias.

GREER GARDENS 128 Goodpasture Island Road, Eugene, OR 97401; (503) 686-8266; catalog $3. From trees to perennials.

HERONSWOOD NURSERY LTD. 7530 NE 228th Street, Kingston, WA 98346-9502; (360) 297-4172; catalog $4. Every new, unusual and choice thing you could ever want to make a garden—or many gardens.

JOY CREEK NURSERY 20300 N.W. Watson Road, Scappoose, OR 97056; (503) 543-7474; catalog $2. Unusual perennials, plus clematis.

PLANT DELIGHTS 9241 Sauls Road, Raleigh, NC 27603; (919) 772-4794; catalog $2. Rarities for the garden, including choice hostas and lots of humor.

RONNIGER'S SEED POTATOES Star Route, Road 73, Moyie Springs, ID 83845; no phone; catalog $1. Certified organic seed potatoes in an incredible diversity of colors, shapes, sizes.

ROSLYN NURSERY 211 Burrs Lane, Dix Hills, NY 11746; (516) 643-9347; catalog $3. Unusual trees and shrubs, plus perennials (especially ones for the woodland).

WELL-SWEEP HERB FARM 317 Mt. Bethel Road, Port Murray, NJ 07865; (908) 852-5390. Herb plants (and seeds) galore.

EQUIPMENT

A.M. LEONARD, INC. P.O. Box 816, 6665 Spiker Road, Piqua, OH 44636-0816; (513) 773-2694; catalog free. One catalog used by professionals that also sells to individuals, for tools and supplies.

GARDENER'S SUPPLY COMPANY 128 Intervale Road, Burlington, VT 05401; (802) 660-3500; catalog free. From tools to pest-fighting gear, aimed at environmentally considerate methods.

LILYPONS WATER GARDENS P.O. Box 10, 6800 Lilypons Lane, Buckeystown, MD 21717; (301) 874-5133; catalog free. From fish to plants to pumps, everything for water gardening.

WALT NICKE COMPANY P.O. Box 433, Topsfield, MA 01983; (800) 822-4114; catalog free. A friendly list of gadgets and tools, from coldframes to pruning shears.

INDEX

Note: Page numbers in **bold** type indicate captions. See Contents (page 12) for specific subjects.